GOOD IS N~~OT ENOUGH~~

KEITH R. WYCHE is the presiden~~t~~ ...ves Management Services (a division ...ty-five-year veteran of Ameritech, A... He is a popular speaker with minorit... ec-ognized for his achievements by *Black Enterprise, Ebony, Crain's Business,* and *Diversity Inc.* magazines. He lives in Scarsdale, New York.

SONIA ALLEYNE is the editorial director of careers and lifestyle for *Black Enterprise.*

✦

Praise for *Good Is Not Enough*

"*Good Is Not Enough* spells out the path for success for those minority professionals who dare to navigate the corporate landscape. Readers would do well to adhere to and fully digest the following unwritten rules: Rule # 1: Read and apply every lesson that Keith Wyche offers. Rule # 2: Never forget rule number one!"
—Dennis Kimbro, author of *Think & Grow Rich: A Black Choice*

"*Good Is Not Enough* is a first-rate book that will undoubtedly change the way minority professionals view and actively approach their careers. Keith Wyche has left no words unwritten to understanding why 'good is not enough.'"   —Lynda M. Dorman, executive director/vice president, BET Foundation, Inc.

"Keith Wyche dispenses the strategies, insights, and dos and don'ts that will bring you to the next level in Corporate America. This book belongs in your briefcase, not on your bookshelf."
—Murray Martin, CEO, Pitney Bowes

"*Good Is Not Enough* could have saved me from bumping into many walls as I traversed corporate America. This book can put you on the fast track for success."   —Quentin L. McCorvey Sr., senior vice president, corporate diversity strategies and programs, KeyBank

"I highly recommend this book—especially for those up-and-coming minority professionals who are attempting to navigate their way through the quirky minefields often found in even the best workplaces in corporate America and globally."   —William W. Wells Jr., chairman of the board, National Black MBA Association

GOOD IS
NOT ENOUGH

—————————— • ——————————

And Other Unwritten Rules
for Minority Professionals

—————————— • ——————————

KEITH R. WYCHE

with Sonia Alleyne

PORTFOLIO

PORTFOLIO
Published by the Penguin Group
Penguin Group (USA) Inc., 375 Hudson Street, New York, New York 10014, U.S.A.
Penguin Group (Canada), 90 Eglinton Avenue East, Suite 700, Toronto, Ontario, Canada M4P 2Y3
(a division of Pearson Penguin Canada Inc.)
Penguin Books Ltd, 80 Strand, London WC2R 0RL, England
Penguin Ireland, 25 St Stephen's Green, Dublin 2, Ireland (a division of Penguin Books Ltd)
Penguin Group (Australia), 250 Camberwell Road, Camberwell, Victoria 3124, Australia
(a division of Pearson Australia Group Pty Ltd)
Penguin Books India Pvt Ltd, 11 Community Centre, Panchsheel Park, New Delhi – 110 017, India
Penguin Group (NZ), 67 Apollo Drive, Rosedale, North Shore 0632, New Zealand
(a division of Pearson New Zealand Ltd)
Penguin Books (South Africa) (Pty) Ltd, 24 Sturdee Avenue, Rosebank, Johannesburg 2196, South Africa

Penguin Books Ltd, Registered Offices:
80 Strand, London WC2R 0RL, England

First published in the United States of America by Portfolio, a member of Penguin Group (USA) Inc. 2008
This paperback edition with a new preface published 2009

1   3   5   7   9   10   8   6   4   2

Copyright © Keith R. Wyche, 2008, 2009
All rights reserved

THE LIBRARY OF CONGRESS HAS CATALOGED THE HARDCOVER EDITION AS FOLLOWS:
Wyche, Keith R.
Good is not enough : and other unwritten rules for minority professionals / Keith R. Wyche.
p. cm.
Includes index.
ISBN 978-1-59184-210-1 (hc.)
ISBN 978-1-59184-291-0 (pbk.)
1. Minority professional employees.   2. Minorities in the professions.   3. Minority executives.
4. Career development.   I. Title.
HD8038.A1W93 2008
650.108—dc22   2008003911

Printed in the United States of America
Set in Minion
Designed by Victoria Hartman

This book is dedicated to my parents,

Leroy (deceased) and Velvet Wyche,

for their unconditional love and unwavering support.

And for never allowing me to settle for just being "good"

when better was obtainable,

and great was within reach!

CONTENTS

Foreword   ix

Preface   xiii

Introduction   1

1. **Corporate Culture Is Critical**
   If You're Going to Play the Game, You'd Better
   Know the Rules   7

2. **Perception Is Pivotal**
   Know How Others See You—Your Brand
   Means Everything   29

3. **Be Visible**
   You Can't Get Ahead If No One Knows Who You Are   40

4. **Know When to Move Over and When to Get Out**
   Taking a Lateral Job versus Leaving Your Company   56

5. **Career Killers You Must Avoid**
   Because Minorities Don't Get Second Chances   85

6. **Must-Have Skills Every Senior Leader Needs**
   And Why They Are Even More Important for Minorities   105

7. **Be More Prepared Than Everyone Else**
   Because Minorities Need to Work Harder to Get Ahead   131

8. **Overcoming Gender Bias**
   The Double Whammy Facing Minority Women   157

9. **Stay Current to Remain Relevant**
   Being a Continuous Learner Is a Must   171

10. **Mentors and Sponsors**
    Why You Need Them and How to Attract Them   186

11. **The Importance of Giving Back**
    "To Whom Much Is Given, Much Is Required"   205

12. **The Importance of Not Giving Up**
    You May Be Closer Than You Think   220

Acknowledgments   228

Further Resources   231

Index   235

FOREWORD

I believe that minorities are at a pivotal point in history. The world is not waiting for us to wake up to our power. It is time for us to take a seat at the table, not only in America but also in the global economy.

As I teach and preach the importance of networking and the building of effective relationships in the African American community, my life's work, I know that each and every day is an opportunity to create a new and powerful story in my culture . . . and unless we find a way to write this new story, to claim our power, there will be devastating implications for our community and for the world. In other words, there is no one to save us—but us! Our excellence is tantamount to our success. This is also true for women, Latinos, and other minority groups striving for excellence in order to get ahead in white America.

More important, I want to point out that there is a distinction between "excellence" and *high personal achievement*. Our capacity for achievement varies according to how well we identify and expand upon our God-given gifts. It is human nature to concentrate on personal achievement as a building block of self-esteem. However, there is a distinction between personal achievement and excellence, not only for blacks but also for women, Latinos, and other minority groups.

As a black man who spent nearly twenty years in corporate America, I have learned that to overcome our failure and to leverage our collective resources for the elevation of all, we must establish excellence as the *overriding perception* of *minorities and the reality for minorities;* in my station, of course, African Americans. But let me make it clear: I believe true excellence comes only when you use your talents and gifts to benefit others *to a greater extent* than you employ those talents for your own personal benefit.

While personal achievement among minorities has helped people of color gain individual independence and confidence, so far it has not significantly contributed to the development of *interdependency* in the African American culture. Blacks must fix that, through excellence! This same "must" applies to other minority groups, through culturally uplifting conduct.

Excellence, by my definition, is the reinvestment of one's unique gifts or personal achievements back into the community in order to improve the human condition within the community. It is my belief also that our generation of minorities must redefine excellence while maintaining high standards of personal achievement. This is our role and contribution. It is also the next step in our respective cultural development. For example: Magic Johnson winning the Most Valuable Player trophy is high personal achievement, but it is not excellence, not at least by my measure. The charitable work of the Magic Johnson Foundation, however, is up to my standard of excellence in the African American community.

The distinction between personal achievement and excellence is important, because it helps us to think of our excellence in communal terms rather than in personal terms, and this leads to another standard for defining our success. It also encourages minorities to create network linkages and to work for the common good, of our people.

I believe that we must have networks of:

- Professionals helping professionals
- Businesses helping professionals
- Professionals helping businesses
- Middle-class and upper-class minorities helping the underclass

Furthermore, you can't have excellence without leadership. And to be a leader is to understand that you must transcend being good at just *functional* and *analytical* (or problem-solving) tasks. You must be able to build relationships that enable you to create a fabric of personal contacts that will provide support, feedback, insight, resources, and information. That's called networking!

Leaders understand that the alternative to effective networking is to fail. You simply will not reach a leadership position, or you will not succeed at leadership, without effective networking skills. Leaders are great networkers and can work effectively with a diverse array of people.

I've seen others who avoided networking, or failed at it because they let interpersonal chemistry, instead of strategic needs, determine which relationships they cultivated. It is a challenge to make the leap from a lifetime of functional contributions and hands-on control to the ambiguous process of building and working through networks.

That said, those individual minorities of means who do not reach down and lift up their own, and are not philanthropic at some level, are socially isolated and ostracized. My point is: in the future, your caring must have more status than your car. We are a long way from that, but I think we are moving toward that idea.

Minorities must be prepared; must create ways to excel in corporate America, other than the status quo. This book, in offering the insights and strategies from those who have "made it" in corporate America, shares how they have moved from personal achievement to excellence.

Good Is Not Enough: And Other Unwritten Rules for Minority Professionals is a must-read for blacks and other minorities facing the reality that in the world of corporate America, the bar is higher, the race is longer, and the prize is harder to hold on to unless you learn how the game is played. Being able to communicate this to the up-and-coming minority corporate executive, or to these who feel stuck in the trenches, is in fact excellence redefined. I commend Keith for his willingness to highlight those who are excelling, and their willingness to share their precious insights for the good of all!

George C. Fraser
Author, *Click: Ten Truths for Building Extraordinary Relationships*

PREFACE

What Minorities in Corporate America Can Learn from President Barack Obama's Success

President Barack Obama's historic achievement has undoubtedly overwhelmed this nation with a wide range of emotions. Who would have imagined just a few years ago that an African American in the primaries would defeat one of the biggest brand names in politics, win a major party's presidential nomination, and then proceed to win the general election, defeating Republican favorite and opponent John McCain by a huge margin?

As we celebrate his success and a historic presidency, what will it really mean for the state of race relations in this country? Although many feel that race relations will improve under an Obama presidency, would it be naive to believe that racism will actually be eradicated—that all glass ceilings will have been permanently shattered?

It certainly won't be the case in corporate America, the field I know best.

Statistics show that most companies still have a long way to go in leveling the playing field for minorities and women, especially in top executive positions. Wage gaps persist between white men and everyone else within the same industries who has equal or higher education levels. Despite the growing number of diversity initiatives and affirmative action programs, it is not an easy goal for minorities to reach senior management. But it is attainable.

What we can learn from those who have made it into C-suite positions—and from President Obama's challenging ascent to the Oval Office—is that a well thought out strategy, a steady focus, the right attitude and a thorough understanding of the rules can make anyone a formidable talent in an organization.

Since President Obama's graduation from Columbia University and his community planning days in the streets of Chicago, he did just about everything right. Here are four of his most effective strategies:

1. Obama crafted, with intention, a winning personal brand. From the introduction of his candidacy to winning the national election, Barack Obama was consistent in his captivating message of change. It was a brilliant platform, because it spoke perfectly to the angst and frustrations of all Americans across racial and economic lines and positioned him as the agent of change. Even as his opponents changed and restructured their political messages, Obama stayed focused and did not waver on what he intended to convey.

The lesson: Perception is critical, because it's reality. Assess your strengths and talents and develop a personal brand around those attributes. Your brand represents what you stand for in business and is developed not just by what you say, but how you perform and the consistency of how you conduct business. Actions not only speak louder than words, they validate who you are and help to shape how you are perceived by your colleagues.

2. Obama was prepared, above and beyond his fellow candidates.

Obama fully understood the rules of the political landscape and developed a variety of strategies that would help him solidify his candidacy during the primaries and eventually win the general election. It is reported that Hilary Clinton admitted not being familiar with how caucuses were run when she lost the Iowa caucus to Obama. He, on the other hand, had learned exactly how the complicated process worked and then developed tactics on how to capture one of the whitest states in the union. It was an important strategy because winning Iowa made him a viable candidate in the eyes of the electorate. It is now acknowledged that his campaign was the best run in political history.

The lesson: Be prepared—more than anyone else. Plain and simple, it's still true that minorities need to work harder than their peers to get ahead. There is no substitute for knowledge, particularly in challenging times. Today's corporate environment won't allow for nonchalance or dispassion. So don't just be on time, be early. Plan in advance. Master the material and know your craft

3. **Obama honed the non-negotiable skills.** It was suggested by many that Obama should have considered a presidential run later in his political career, but he realized that the time was right to mount his campaign of hope and change. Not only was he able to stay focused on his goal even when the odds seemed stacked against him, Obama was able to engage and inspire many even in the midst of crisis. He remained emotionally, mentally, and spiritually centered, particularly during the presidential debates even while being personally attacked and referred to as "naive" and "That One." In the end viewers who were polled on each candidate's performance maintained that they saw Obama as more "presidential." Obama also leveraged new technology and viral marketing with grassroots organizing to reach, connect, and galvanize a new group of constituents that had never really been previously courted by the electoral process.

The lesson: Some skills are non-negotiable. To advance to the highest ranks in corporate America, every leader must demonstrate certain traits: (1) *strategic visioning*—the insight to recognize a limited window of opportunity when it presents itself. (2) *Authentic leadership*—the ability to engage and energize others, even when faced with personal and professional challenges, including prejudice. (3) *Awareness/political judgment*—the ability to successfully navigate organizational boundaries, to understand trends and nuances across business units and geographic boundaries.

4. Obama proactively and strategically engaged mentors and sponsors. Many people may not realize the extent to which Obama found champions and allies to pave the way for his success. Before his run for the U.S. Senate, he engaged a group of well-informed and well-connected advisers in business and politics, beyond the African American community. His choice of Vice President Joe Biden (experienced in political world affairs), as well as his cabinet choices further demonstrates his wisdom in selecting strong political partners and advisers who complement and enhance his overall effectiveness.

The lesson: You can't do it alone. The single most important thing an individual—particularly a minority—can do to advance his or her career is secure a team of advisers. You must seek out, engage, and enlist the support of those who are proven winners in the corporate game. Some will be mentors; others will be part of your network, but they are the experienced players who will help you decode the unwritten rules of your company and assist you in developing a strategic plan for winning.

With his ascent to the highest office in the land and the most powerful in the world, President Obama's success has left an indelible imprint in the world of politics and business. If you heed his lessons, there are aspiring chief executives like you who could inspire great changes for corporate America as well.

Introduction

First, let me begin by saying, thank you for making the decision to purchase this book. My guess is, you are a young minority professional who has career aspirations that have not yet been met, and you are looking for some pearls of wisdom that will help you in your quest. Perhaps you are at the other end of the spectrum, and find yourself a frustrated minority working in the business world, your career stuck in a rut. You can't seem to get promoted, no matter how well you perform. You've tried unsuccessfully to identify a mentor to help guide your career and provide you the guidance you so desperately need, but to no avail. You are beginning to feel like no matter what you do, no matter how hard you work, you are destined to go unrecognized, unappreciated, and unrewarded. Let me tell you, you are not alone. Many years ago I had an idea for a completely different book. Instead of writing a book that focused on how to overcome the obstacles, I found myself in a very different place. Like some of you, I found myself burned out, frustrated, and confused.

The introduction that I had prepared for that yet-unpublished book gives you an idea of how dire my situation was:

Introduction: "What Lack I Yet?"

After much internal debate and rationalization, I have decided that this is a book that had to be written. Not for the sake of adding yet another book dealing with the subject of hitting "glass ceilings" to the shelves of bookstores, but rather as a therapeutic exercise for the author. I have always been a believer that if feelings of anger, rage, or hostility are suppressed and not dealt with openly and honestly, the result can be one of devastation for both the oppressed and the oppressor.

Initially, I felt that the frustrations that I experience almost on a daily basis were mine alone and not representative of what my minority professional brothers and sisters had to cope with. Surprisingly enough, after meeting other minority professionals through the years and being associated with various minority professional organizations, I found that I was not alone. On the surface we all looked successful. Many of us enjoyed the trappings of success—nice homes, nice cars, and the like. But few of us ever really seemed complete. We identified ourselves by our titles and our corporations. "Hi, I'm Stan Young, an accountant with XYZ Company" was a typical introduction. Business cards were passed around like baseball cards and the more impressive the title, the better. However, something happened on the way to the boardroom.

During the economic recession of the late 1980s and early '90s, many black professionals found they had been taken off the fast track, had their careers put on hold, or worse yet, been taken out of the game altogether. They had been invited to the party late, then asked to leave early. Phrases like *right-sizing*, *downsizing*, and *the needs of the business* were given as reasons (or excuses) as to why the party was over. At the same time, they watched others within these same organizations not only survive but be given opportunities for success that these minority professionals could only dream of.

Today, the question that thousands of minority professionals are asking both themselves and those who claim to provide them with career opportunities is, What lack I yet? As a direct result of the civil rights movement of the late 1960s, black America has produced its most qualified, educated generation of professionals in modern history. These professionals, armed with their degrees and ambitions, descended upon corporate America full of hopes, dreams, and promises. Hopes of being all that their parents and grandparents could not be, thanks to the limited opportunities provided them by a blatantly racist society. Dreams of sharing the American dream of "life, liberty and the pursuit of happiness." Most of all, promises of equal opportunity, "careers" versus "jobs," and above all, acceptance.

Now, decades later, many of these professionals (the author included) find themselves angry, frustrated, burned out, and otherwise demoralized. They have played the game, only to find out that the game has been changed, and they themselves have been played. While it could be argued that most if not all of these young minority professionals enjoy a standard of living and quality of life that far surpasses that of their forefathers, they have paid a tremendous price in return. They have been forced to assimilate, hide their blackness, and basically deny themselves for what amounts to the crumbs that have fallen from the table, while still asking, "What lack I yet?" And what we have found is that "selling out" is no guarantee of acceptance. In fact, hopefully, it is not an option.

It is not the aim of this author to present this book as an analytical study of the trials and tribulations of the black professional, or attempt to speak for all minority professionals in general. Rather, this is an attempt to express the feelings and issues faced by many minority professionals in white corporate America.

This book serves to share the concerns of those who tread this lonesome path, to let others learn from their mistakes while at the same time providing a vehicle for self-examination. For many, this was a chosen path. We chose to try and "fit in." We chose to wear the Brooks Brothers suits and the Ann Taylor outfits. We decided to join the "right clubs," to live in the "right neighborhoods," and, most important, to say the "right things." We wanted the whole world, and all it had to offer. Some have realized their goals; others are still striving, and many have given up. But all have had to wrestle with yet another question: "What does a man (or woman) profit, to gain the whole world, and to lose his own soul?"

As you can probably tell after reading my thoughts at the time, I was bitter and upset. I was a director of sales, managing a team of sales reps, and had just lost out to a majority candidate hired from outside. This was particularly frustrating because after losing out to an internal candidate for a similar job a short time earlier, I created a development plan with my vice president to better prepare me when the next opportunity became available. After getting the call from my VP informing me that once again I had not gotten the job, I felt betrayed and lied to. I had done everything that was asked of me. I was a top performer, I spent my nights for two years earning an MBA, and I felt I deserved better—better from my manager and VP, better from my company, and better from society at large. I was determined to press the matter, confront those who were blocking my way, and, more important, *make* my company treat me fairly. However, during a moment of reflection, I asked myself a question: What happens if I take all this frustration and confront my boss and my company about what they aren't doing, and nothing changes? Furthermore, I was forced to consider another question: Even if I left company A for company B, what guarantee would I have that I would not run into the same issues and concerns that I found at my previous employer?

Lastly, I had to take an honest look at myself, not only focusing on my strengths, but identifying areas that needed development. Is it possible that while I did possess skills in one area, I was ill prepared in others? Had I really done all that I could to position myself for success? Had I made enough of an effort to develop relationships with key senior leaders, or others who could influence the hiring decision? However, my real liberation came when I realized that while there were definitely things my company could do to help me advance in my career, I really had little power to make them do anything. However, I had complete control over what I could do for myself! Armed with a new determination, I set out not to change corporate America, but to understand how I needed to change my behavior, approach, and image to better position myself for success. This began my ten-year journey from director of sales to division president of a Fortune 500 company. This transformation didn't come about because my IQ suddenly jumped to Mensa status. It didn't happen because overnight, senior management decided they liked me. It happened because I came to realize there was a process to getting recognized, rewarded, and promoted. It happened because I came to understand what to look for, and what to avoid when considering a potential employer. And it happened because I took the time, effort, and energy to develop myself in areas that would make me a more attractive candidate for advancement.

This book is my effort to share with others some of the key lessons learned by myself and others who have reached a certain level of success in the business world. Many of these lessons will sound familiar, and a few may offer a unique perspective. However, it is my hope that as the reader, you will walk away with at least one idea, suggestion, or thought that can help enhance your career. And then, after achieving success in your given field, you can take time to move beyond success to significance by sharing your lessons with others.

1

Corporate Culture Is Critical

If You're Going to Play the Game,
You'd Better Know the Rules

How well do you *really* know your company? You know its history, products, and services, the management team, board of directors, their fiscal budget and expansion plans for growing markets. You know your job description—and are confident in your ability to perform the task. There may have been several reasons why you joined this firm: the salary increase, the director or VP title you so highly coveted, an attractive sign-on bonus, or the opportunity to work in a prime metropolitan location. Whatever the draw, you believe that this is an opportunity for you to grow professionally. But, again, how well do you know your firm?

It is important for aspiring professionals to understand that companies have a business reputation as well as a manner in which they do business. Before you can even begin to seriously address the advancement of your career from your present position, you have to be able to assess how your performance will be perceived—and n this company. To make that assessment, you have

re than revenues and stats, you must know and under-

ulture—how the organization functions in terms of ideology, protocol, and etiquette. The behaviors that result from these areas are a company's unwritten code of conduct—the rules of the game. Working for a corporation is analogous to playing professional sports. Regardless of the sport, to be successful, you have to understand the rules.

HOW WELL ARE WE PLAYING THE GAME TODAY?

There is no denying that in almost every avenue of life, minorities have made tremendous progress. The number of minority coaches in professional sports has increased. Players in both Major League Baseball and the National Basketball Association are predominantly Latino and African American, respectively. The 2007 NFL Super Bowl game featured two African American coaches. The number of minority mayors, congress members, and other political positions is noteworthy. Therefore, it would be reasonable to assume that with all the gains minorities have made in recent years, the corporate world would show similar progress. From a boardroom perspective, the number of minority CEOs has increased significantly over the past fifteen years. In 1995, there were no people of color serving as CEOs of a Fortune 500 company. As recently as 2005 there were at least fifteen African American, Latino, or Asian leaders holding this title. In the fall of 2007, two of the country's most highly visible minority CEOs, Stanley O'Neal of Merrill Lynch and Richard Parsons of Time Warner/AOL, announced their resignations. In January 2008, Aylwin Lewis stepped down as CEO of Sears Holdings, created after the merger of Kmart and Sears. While it was disappointing to lose three such talented leaders, even with their resignations, there remain at least four African American, four Latino, five Asian, and thirteen women who serve as CEOs of Fortune 500 companies, according to *DiversityInc* magazine.* However, there is still room for improvement in the overall number of minorities working in key positions within major corporations.

Let's take a look at the facts:

Executive Representation of Women and Minorities in Corporate America

• According to the Bureau of Labor Statistics Division of Labor Force Statistics for 2006, there were 1,689 total chief executives employed in the United States in the category of "management, business, and financial operations," of which 23.4 percent were women, 4.6 percent were Latino, 3.9 percent were Asian, and 3.1 percent were African American. In this study, "chief executives" are defined as follows: they determine and formulate policies and provide the overall direction of companies or private and public sector organizations within the guidelines set up by a board of directors or similar governing body; and they plan, direct, or coordinate operational activities at the highest level of management with the help of subordinate executives and staff managers.†

• According to Catalyst, a nonprofit research organization, women hold 50.3 percent of all management and professional positions, but make up less than 2 percent of CEOs at Fortune 500 and Fortune 1000 publicly traded companies.‡

---

* "Why Are So Few CEOs Women and People of Color?," *DiversityInc*, November 2007.

† U.S. Department of Labor, Bureau of Labor Statistics, "Employed Persons by Detailed Occupation, Sex, Race, and Hispanic or Latino Ethnicity," 2006.

‡ "Study Shows Women of Color Held Back by Discrimination," *Black Enterprise*, May 2006. http://www.blackenterprise.com/ArchiveOpen.asp?Source=ArchiveTab/2006/03/030627.htm.

- For black women, the figures are dismal: they constitute a mere 1.1 percent of corporate officers and top earners. White males, on the other hand, make up 98 percent of CEOs and 95 percent of the top earners of the five hundred largest publicly traded companies.[*]

- According to the Bureau of Labor Statistics Division of Labor Force Statistics, there were 19 million executives, managers, and administrators in the U.S. labor force in 1998. Of that number, 7.2 percent were black. In 1988, only 5.6 percent of the nation's executives, managers, and administrations were African American; by 1991 that number had grown slightly, to 5.7 percent.[†]

- Despite considerable progress, black representation at the top of corporate America still falls woefully short. While African Americans make up 13 percent of the U.S. population, they hold just 8 percent (about 260 of roughly 3,200) of the board seats at the nation's top publicly traded companies, according to the Executive Leadership Council, a nonprofit organization of black executives devoted to broadening black leadership. And only 2 percent of those seats are held by black women.[‡]

- While just a fraction of board seats are occupied by blacks today, about 90 percent or more of the largest companies in the consumer goods, finance, health care, and transportation industries have at least one black director. Recruiters like Charles Tribbett note that corporate boards have often expressed concern that they simply don't know where to find qualified African American board candidates. That's why a select group, including Richard Parsons and Ariel's John W. Rogers, Jr., sit on multiple boards.[§]

---

[*] Ibid.

[†] "The Top 50 Blacks in Corporate America," *Black Enterprise*, February 2000. http://www.findarticles.com/p/articles/mi_m1365/is_7_30/ai_58916297.

[‡] "Seeking Diversity in the Boardroom," *BusinessWeek*, December 18, 2006. http://www.businessweek.com/magazine/content/06_51/b4014073.htm?chan=search.

[§] Ibid.

WHOEVER OWNS THE COURT MAKES THE RULES

When I was an inner-city kid growing up in the 1970s, playing ball was the neighborhood pastime. Long before Sony PlayStations and Nintendo, most summer days were spent playing sandlot baseball, backyard basketball, or street football. I loved basketball. As a kid, I would play "21" with the older boys. Instead of being team-centered, the game was an individual challenge of each player's skills on the court against the other players. The winner was the first one to reach twenty-one points.

The real challenge, however, with backyard basketball was that the rules and the boundaries of the game changed depending on whose yard it was. The foul line might move, the basket height was often adjusted, and the out-of-bounds markers seemed to change depending on who had the ball. In a nutshell, whoever owned the court made the rules! If the court's owner was losing, he could modify the game in his favor. One day as I was about to win my first game with the older boys, the court's owner, who was a bank-shot wizard, declared that to win the game, the final shot *had* to be a bank shot. And if you missed it, you had to go back to zero points. I didn't win that game. But he taught me a valuable lesson: **Make sure you know the rules BEFORE you enter the court!**

This point is obviously more critical in corporate America, particularly since the idiosyncrasies of a corporation are far less obvious than those of childhood court buddies. But they do exist across all industries and business types and sizes, and create the culture that defines the game. In a very broad sense, general assessments of culture can be made about various industries, many of which most professionals already know. For instance, banking and finance have a tendency to be conservative and formal. On the other hand, high-tech organizations and media companies tend to be more liberal in both dress code and manner of operation. Utility companies have historically supported an "entitlement" culture based on seniority when it comes to internal promotions, whereas most sales organizations tend to promote and reward based on individual performance.

It's at the micro level that many professionals get stumped. Each organization within a given industry will have its own culture, and for you to thrive within that organization, it is essential that you determine as best you can what that culture is—and if it is a good fit for you! Many careers stall and stagnate because the individual stayed in a particular job with little to no understanding of the company culture, which can range from the use of administrative employees to involvement in company social events. How are ideas received? How is creativity expressed? How is performance rewarded? How is influence measured? Are certain divisions of the company regarded more highly than others? Does the CEO schedule periodic meetings with all of the affinity groups? How important is the company softball game, Christmas party, or annual gathering at a senior executive's summer home?

✦ *Bobbie's Story:*
A Quick Lesson in Corporate Culture

When newly hired attorney Bobbie was invited to a weekend event at a country club by the firm's partners, she assumed the invite was optional and decided not to attend. Several days later the partners approached her about her absence and encouraged her to attend future events. Although they never even suggested that the event was mandatory, their approach made Bobbie nervous, and she sought the advice of a senior associate to help her decipher the message. The truth was, she was expected to be there, and because she was one of very few African Americans in the firm, her absence was very noticeable.

HOW DOES CORPORATE CULTURE AFFECT CAREER ADVANCEMENT?

One of the most frequent questions I'm asked by minority managers who want to advance their careers is related to understanding and navigating corporate culture. I am regularly approached by employees asking for advice, who are struggling with situations like this: "I'm doing okay at the company I work for, but I'm just not getting ahead; it's not happening for me there. Should I try to make myself fit into this culture, or should I just move on, and try to find a company where I would fit in better from the start?" Many people are reluctant to take that step and leave their current employer in search of something new, so they often stay in a frustrating environment where typically, if it's the wrong cultural fit, it's also the wrong fit for getting ahead. But there are two sides here. Employees who struggle with environmental climate do so because of these two reasons:

- Incompatibility or a clash of values
- Not fully understanding the rules in the beginning

Bobbie may have made a misstep by not attending her partners' gathering, but a senior-level manager alerted her to the political ramifications of such a professional faux pas. She received help and support—or coaching—from a "player" in the game. That's why finding a mentor—a senior-level, highly respected influencer—should be your first priority upon starting at a company. Waiting, or trying to figure it out on your own, may lead to frustration and irreparable damage that could derail your potential opportunities at your company if you continue to make costly behavioral mistakes.

Of course, if you realize that there is a misalignment between your goals and values and how the company responds to your working style and performance, then it is important to make plans to leave. In a later chapter we will discuss in greater detail how to determine if you should stay with a company, take a lateral position within that company, or just flat-out leave! But please know that nothing is more demoralizing, frustrating, and downright burdensome than to remain in a job or with a company that does not value, respect, or reward your hard work in making them successful! Life is too short to wake up every day knowing that the value you bring to a company is underappreciated.

IT'S MORE THAN JUST SALARY AND TITLE

Several years ago, I was working as a general manager at Ameritech's headquarters in Chicago. I had grown up in the Bell System, having started my career in 1981 with Ohio Bell Telephone Company and, later, AT&T Communications. After a rocky start and years of top performance, I was well known, respected, and had a career trajectory that involved a promotion roughly every two years. However, in late 1999 the company was acquired by its Baby Bell sibling SBC Communications (now AT&T again). During the transition process, I interviewed and was offered either a lateral assignment that would have required me to relocate to SBC headquarters in San Antonio, Texas, or a hefty separation package.

Because I was not known or well positioned in the SBC organization, and my mentors were no longer in place, I opted for the separation package.

For the first time in my professional career, I was without a job! Not only that, but this was in the middle of the "dot-bomb" nightmare, and the job market had all but dried up, especially for minorities. Afraid that it would take months to find another high-visibility six-figure position, I immediately began my job search. Through networking (which is a must for every minority), I was able to land what appeared to be an ideal job as VP of sales for an industry-leading outsourced billing and customer care solutions provider. The salary was acceptable, the sign-on bonus reasonable, and the culture *seemed* to be fine. During the interview process, the CEO told me that they were committed to diversity, encouraged creativity, and rewarded results. They were located in Cincinnati—not an ideal location for me, but I needed a job.

It took less than a month to realize that while this was an excellent company, it was not a great fit culturally for me. Yes, they had a well-paid, highly skilled sales organization, but it was an operations-driven company! The senior leadership team consisted primarily of executives with strong operations backgrounds, most of the company's value proposition was rooted in "operational excellence," and the sales organization could not even propose a solution without the formal approval of the operations department. Operations called the shots and ran the show. Sales was merely a distribution channel that contributed to the company's growth, but had zero influence on major decisions.

Additionally, I later discovered several company rituals, such as required donations to the chairman's favorite charity and donating to a political action committee. Was there anything wrong with this culture? Absolutely not! They were and still are a highly respected, highly profitable company in their space. The problem was, the manner in which they conducted business was not a good fit for me.

HOW WILL I BENEFIT FROM MY DEDICATION AND PERFORMANCE?

One of the first determinations that you need to make regarding cultural fit has to do with how the company recognizes and rewards its leaders. The means and methods by which leaders are recognized and rewarded have a direct correlation to how you will or will not be recognized and rewarded. And to the extent that you understand this, your career has great potential to blossom and grow, or wither and die.

In an ideal world, a manager is paid, promoted, and rewarded based solely on his or her performance or the performance of his or her team. Typically, each year you will be given a documented set of goals and objectives to focus your efforts. Most often, at the end of the year, you will be rated on a scale of 1 to 5; for example, a 3 means you met the objectives, a 1 indicates you significantly exceeded the objectives, and a 5 means it's time to find another job. The goal should be to show consistency by achieving above-average performance ratings year after year. By doing so, you will increase the probability that you are considered for increased responsibility; at a minimum, you will have demonstrated that you have *earned* the right to be considered.

PERFORMANCE VERSUS SENIORITY

Unfortunately, many minorities do not work in an ideal world. In fact, minorities are always expected to exceed objectives. But depending on the work environment, the quality of your job performance may have less influence than you might expect on how you rise through the ranks in your company. As stated previously, early in my career I worked for Ohio Bell, part of the AT&T family prior to the organization's being divested in 1983. It was a proud, stable company with a utility company culture and a union mindset; customer service was not always a priority, and workers were ranked based more on seniority than on performance. Additionally, it was a virtual monopoly, with little industry competition. After a few successful years of selling, I decided to apply for a sales manager position. I was informed, however, that because I had held my job for only three years, I was ineligible to apply for a manager's position. The minimum "time in title" was five years. Unmoved, I decided to take the next two years to get my MBA through an evening and weekend program. After my fifth year in the company, having earned my MBA, I applied again for the sales manager position. This time, I was given an interview, but the job was given to an older salesman who, though he had no degree at all, did have ten years of service. It was a valuable lesson, and I vowed never again to work for a company where seniority trumped performance!

HOW MUCH DOES SIZE MATTER?

There can be vast differences in how a company operates, depending on whether it has a small or large company culture. Nathan, a friend and colleague of mine, got a firsthand look at how different the two can be. For most of his career, Nathan worked for two of the largest players in the overnight shipping business. He enjoyed the perks that came with working for a company with deep pockets: the corporate suites, the latest technology, expensive recognition trips, and a travel expense budget that allowed him to enjoy the finest accommodations when traveling on company business.

This all changed when Nathan joined a much smaller, family-run company. Almost immediately, he realized just how different his work life had become. The company suite was reserved for the owner's friends and family; laptops were handed down from one person to the next; instead of four- or five-star accommodations, he was advised to stay at quality budget hotels. He also realized that decision-making was limited to a small group of individuals who were either family members or longtime family friends. Since he was neither, he was left out of the inner circle.

There can, however, be advantages to working in smaller firms. Small companies can be less bureaucratic, more informal, and more open to a variety of new ideas and business solutions. Because small companies often require more multitasking across disciplines, depending on their culture, they may give you opportunities to grow and develop at a rate and in ways that may not be available to you in a larger, more structured environment.

The first step, however, in controlling and guiding your career is understanding the politics of your environment. Some of that can be determined on the outside—before you join. The following are certain steps to consider, and questions to ask *before* signing your offer letter.

COACHING TIPS

Be sure to understand where you best fit in. Take a good, hard look at yourself, and inventory your strengths and weaknesses and what you're willing to do to fit in and advance your career. For example, will you thrive in a fast-paced environment? Are you willing to "go along to get along," even if it means engaging in company rituals and events that have little or no interest to you, such as attending all social functions and supporting the CEO's favorite charities? Will you be comfortable in an environment in which, despite diversity efforts, employees are still insensitive and/or uncomfortable about how to treat those who are different from them? For a bigger paycheck, are you willing to work in a company where respect for the individual is secondary to profit, "groupthink," or a company-comes-first culture?

This rule even applies at the CEO level. In 2005 Aylwin Lewis, then president and CEO of YUM Brands (Pizza Hut, KFC, Taco Bell, Long John Silver's), left after thirteen years of being the highest-ranking African American in restaurant history, to become president and CEO of Kmart. However, before making his move, Lewis took time to make sure it was a good cultural fit. He stated regarding his new role, "I would not have left the situation at YUM Brands to come to a company that was not interested in being a growth company, in winning in the marketplace and operating great stores to serve unmet company needs."

Research through sources such as the Internet and consumer and trade periodicals to gain insights on the company. You can obtain a significant amount of information regarding a potential employer.

- Is it considered a "great place to work" by any leading business publications?
- Has it won any awards for diversity?
- Do members of the board as well as the senior leadership of the organization consist of people who look like you?

- Is it affiliated with, or does it support or endorse, professional and social organizations that are meaningful to you, such as NAACP, National Black MBA Association (NBMBAA), National Society of Hispanic MBAs (NSHMBA), or Women in Business?

Search the company Web site and, if it is publicly held, read its annual report. What do managers say about themselves? An organization, like an individual, will usually share its most shining accomplishments.

- Do they talk about their diversity efforts and outside recognition for those efforts?
- What do they focus on the most in their annual report? Has the company recently undergone a merger or acquisition? How has the stock performed over the past few years? If they have been underperforming financially, are they in a cost-cutting mode?
- In particular, what does the chairman focus on in his/her highlights? Typically, the CEO will outline the top three or more corporate initiatives for the upcoming year. This can prove to be vital information when interviewing and provide tremendous insights into the company's culture.

Certain questions should be asked at various stages of the interview process. I would not recommend these questions for the initial interview, but during later stages of the interview process, the following questions may provide additional insight about a company's culture.

DIVERSITY
- Tell me about your diversity efforts to date.
- Do you provide diversity training for your managers?

- What percentage of your middle/senior management is minority?
- What outside organizations do you support or endorse, or are you affiliated with?
- Does the CEO support affinity groups?

COMPENSATION/PROMOTIONS

- What is the average length of time between promotions for individuals who perform well?
- What happened to the person who most recently held this position?
- If promoted, how long was she in the role?
- If demoted or dismissed, how much time was she given to succeed?

Recently I received a call from an executive search firm working for a multinational bank recruiting for a C-level (CEO, CFO, CIO) position. Somewhat intrigued, I agreed to meet with the search firm executive to discuss the opportunity in greater detail. However, prior to our meeting, I went to the Internet and researched the bank from a diversity perspective. One of the first things I discovered was that although they had roughly forty individuals identified as "officers," there was not a single African American male listed, and only one African American female. Ironically, they dedicated an entire section of their Web site to highlighting their diversity accomplishments, and in fairness, they did have a great track record in outwardly supporting minority organizations and community involvement in disadvantaged neighborhoods. However, when it came down to the senior leadership team, it was not representative of their customer base. Later I decided not to pursue this opportunity, in part because I sensed the internal culture was not one that I could thrive in.

Check the "network." Throughout the book, I will repeat this often: Never underestimate the power of networking. The best source for information on understanding and navigating through the corporate culture of a new organization is your professional network. Very often, if your network is broad enough, you will discover that someone within your network either knows or has contact with someone who knows or is connected to the organization you are inquiring about. Nothing is more valuable than inside information.

Not long ago I learned that a former IBM colleague was a final candidate for a VP position at Pitney Bowes. Although he was interested in the job, he was not fully comfortable with what he perceived the culture to be at the company. Once we connected, I gave him the "inside scoop." That information helped give him a better perspective on the company's real expectations, and he felt more confident about his decision to join the company.

While there will always be some unwritten rules you will only discover *after* you start the job, one way to more quickly decipher corporate codes and reduce professional blunders is to identify a mentor early on.

RULES TO REMEMBER

You must be willing to put in the work! While this should be a given, it is always prudent to be reminded that nothing will ever take the place of doing the work. Whether you call it working *hard* or working *smart*, the reality of today's workplace is that success in a field crowded with talent requires that you take the time, effort, and energy needed to excel in your role. Too often, people want the rewards of success without the effort. When you are a minority, it is not enough to just be good! Good will keep you employed. Good may even garner you a raise or two. But if your goals are higher than just being mediocre, then you must be willing to make the sacrifices necessary to reach the top, whether that means pursuing an advanced degree, taking courses to improve your performance in a given area, or just plain outworking and outthinking your fellow coworkers. If climbing the corporate ladder is what you desire, be prepared to do what it takes to ascend each step.

It is not a level playing field. It would be nice to assume that after the civil rights movement, after years of affirmative action, after all the diversity efforts, the playing field has been leveled. The truth of the matter is, even in this new millennium an imbalance remains. While much has improved over the past decades regarding the inclusion of minorities in the business world, as the statistics cited earlier in this chapter make clear, there is still room for improvement. As companies learn to truly embrace diversity and the business value that it brings, more and more minorities will receive the opportunity to assume positions of authority and leadership. Examples abound of companies that understand this: General Electric, Bank of America, Target, and Pitney Bowes, just to name a few. However, until the Top 50 Best Places for Minorities to Work list becomes the Top 1,000 Best Places for Minorities to Work, there will always be a challenge. The real challenge is not using this reality as an excuse to fail or to remain average, but rather understanding it, and even challenging it, and succeeding in spite of it.

It's not about what the company should do, but what you should do! Don't fall victim to thinking that the *company* should be doing more for you. While I do believe that any company that truly understands both the social and economic benefits of hiring, developing, and promoting diverse talent will certainly take steps to invest in that talent, the responsibility is not theirs solely. As a minority professional, you have a personal responsibility and a moral obligation to develop your God-given skills to the best of your ability, and to leverage them for your own personal growth. Have you taken the time to further your education or enhance your skills? Have you developed relationships with key leaders in the company and shared with them your career aspirations? Have you identified what assignments or roles you believe will best help you develop and move to the next level? When was the last time you created a personal development plan? Never forget that in the end, you are the author, architect, and owner of your career! It's up to you to make it happen!

Never let anyone limit your vision of what you can accomplish. By now, we've all heard the stories of people who refused to let others define them or what they could accomplish—Michael Jordan being cut from his high school basketball team, Jennifer Lopez being told she would never be more than a "fly-girl" dancer, Yao Ming being warned he couldn't compete at the NBA level, or Venus and Serena Williams being mocked for learning to play tennis on the inner-city tennis courts of Compton. The list could go on and on. While these professionals achieved against all odds in the world of sports and entertainment, the same could be said for the Richard Parsonses, Ken Chenaults, Ann Fudges, and Linda Alvarezes of the corporate world.

The truth is, there will always be those in the crowd who will try to set limits on what you as a minority can achieve, who you can become, and how far you can go in the corporate world. These voices will whisper that you aren't polished enough, that you didn't graduate from the right school, or that you shouldn't even try for that open director, VP, or president position. I encourage you to ignore those voices. Instead, listen to your own voice, and the voices of your ancestors who encouraged you to "dare to dream." Find a company that values your potential and gives you the opportunity to excel. Refuse to remain in a role, a department, or a company that, after you've demonstrated you can achieve, will not recognize and reward your achievements. And above all, never lose faith in yourself and what you can achieve. In his song "Dare to Dream," musician Onaje Allan Gumbs reminds us, "Our wings were made for the sky, and no matter what, we must fly."

Always **have an exit strategy.** While in most cases you would never go into any company or role with the anticipation of leaving, the reality is, you have taken this job or assignment with certain career goals in mind:

- To develop a new skill.
- To utilize skills you have, but are not using in your current role.
- To gain experience managing a profit-and-loss (P&L) statement.
- To increase your span of control by managing a larger pool of employees.

While your primary objective is to accomplish one of the above, at some point you are expecting to leverage this experience and move on to a new role, earn a promotion, or at a minimum, increase your income. But what happens if you don't? Assuming you are performing at a level that meets or exceeds expectations, how long are you willing to wait for that next opportunity?

What is an "exit strategy"? Encarta defines an exit strategy as "a means of escaping one's current situation, typically an unfavourable situation. An organization or individual without an exit strategy may be in a quagmire. At worst, an exit strategy will save face; at best, an exit strategy will peg a withdrawal to the achievement of an objective worth more than the cost of continued involvement."

This whole notion of an exit strategy was something I first practiced by accident. In the mid-1980s I left AT&T to work for IBM. The world was moving toward voice and data integration. Companies were putting plans in place to implement integrated digital services networks (ISDNs), and computer technology and local area networks (LANs) were becoming commonplace. I decided to enhance my telephone-industry skills by working for IBM and learning the data-processing end of the business. I entered IBM with a plan. Knowing that I would have to at some point go back to being a sales rep and "carry a bag" to have any credibility at Big Blue, I took a job as an advisory account rep. The goal was to have two to three successful years as a rep, move into a staff role for a year, and eventually become a marketing manager, then a branch manager.

However, though I had earned multiple 100% Clubs and been rated highly every year, promotions were few and far between. In the spring of 1993, after six years in various sales roles, I met with both my business unit executive and my area general manager to discuss my concerns. I was told I was on the radar for a promotion, but needed more time in my current job. I told my business unit executive that either he would promote me in the next six months, or I would promote myself! He chuckled, not sure what to make of my comment. However, what I was really saying to him was, "I have a track record of success, I've been in this role longer than others you have promoted without such a restriction, and just in case you don't honor your word, I am now actively seeking employment elsewhere." From that day, I began to work with search firms, and eventually through a chance meeting ran into my old boss from AT&T, who offered me a job at Ameritech in November 1993 in Detroit. The ironic thing is, once I gave my two weeks' notice, within days my manager presented me with three positions I could be promoted to. Unfortunately, I had emotionally and mentally disconnected, and my exit strategy had been implemented.

TIPS ON CREATING AN EXIT STRATEGY

- Determine what it is you want to gain out of this new job, assignment, or experience. (See examples above.)
- Define what success in this new role looks like to your superiors, and as best you can determine, how long it will take to demonstrate that success with some consistency.
- Try to gain an understanding up front from your superiors on how long they expect you to remain in this role before they consider you for promotion, assuming you are exceeding expectations.
- Create a timeline, allowing for a nine-to-eighteen-month buffer, based on your expectations and feedback from your superiors, on when you should be moving on to your next role. (Depending on the company's culture, this could be anywhere from two to four years.)
- Detail what your actions will be if the new role, promotion, or assignment does not materialize in that time frame. (For example, work with search firms, sign up for Monster.com, or attend professional-level career fairs.)
- If the time frame is exceeded, implement the exit strategy.

COACHING TIP

In conclusion, it's your responsibility to know the game in which you are about to play. You should do your best to understand the culture, but never enter an organization expecting to change it. Get in, learn the rules, get to know the players, follow the instruction of the coaches, then go on to be the Most Valuable Player! But if you choose to try and play the game outside the corporate rules and without proper coaching, you could land on the bench, or be cut from the team! And remember, whether you feel you need it or not, always have an exit strategy that allows you to land on your feet.

2

Perception Is Pivotal

Know How Others See You—
Your Brand Means Everything

In early 2000, when Aetna faced grave financial troubles, the board had installed a new CEO who had never run a for-profit company. Knowing his limitations, he informed human resources that the company needed a "nuts and bolts" person to revive the struggling insurance company. The headhunter they employed replied that the best man for the job was Ronald A. Williams, an African American executive known as an expert in the intricacies of health-care management and with a reputation of being a turnaround king earned by having revived Wellpoint, a California-based health-care company.

Williams, who had already left the health management industry, decided to accept the offer to be Aetna's chief medical officer in 2001, and in a few years was able to increase the company's stock by 700 percent. Today he is president, chairman, and CEO.

Aside from being a smart, hardworking, and well-liked professional, Williams is known by colleagues and industry professionals as an executive who intimately understands what drives the managed health industry. He is also known as a problem solver—which in the case of Wellpoint and Aetna contributed significantly to profitable growth. It is all part of his personal brand. What are colleagues saying about you?

How others perceive you and the value you bring to an organization will have an enormous impact on your career advancement. It is a common misconception that performance alone determines who gets the corner office. In reality, how you distinguish yourself from your peers, how that behavior is perceived by those in the senior ranks, and how you actually manage that perception is a critical part of the process for advancement. Too often, minority professionals do not spend enough time and effort on what messages they send about themselves through the work they perform.

Today, the term *personal branding* is used to describe the process of creating and managing how you are perceived when your name is mentioned for committees, projects, boards, or promotions. Just as certain perceptions come to mind when you hear "Lexus" or "Yugo" in the automotive realm, the mention of your name in your company, and in your industry, has a value attached to it. The question is: How much currency does it get?

. . .

Whether you consider it or not, everyone has a personal brand—one that is being managed, or one that simply exists. The most successful professionals, however, are intimately involved in creating and managing their brands. Of course, many minorities battle with the idea of perception regularly. In many cases, our focus has been to offset long-held stereotypical perceptions about our ability and talent— but branding goes beyond proving that we can do the work. It is also broader than gaining acceptance and being well liked. Some may conclude, "If my superiors like me, they will have a good perception of me." Your personal brand speaks more to an expectation. It is important to be liked, but it is more valuable to be respected for the type of work you deliver, the manner in which it is always performed, and the results you yield consistently. When you are recruited to a new position, job, board position, or committee project, your colleagues know what to expect, and they place a high value on that expectation.

WHAT MAKES UP YOUR BRAND?

When I discuss the idea of perception with young minority professionals, their initial focus is on their outward appearance. Comments typically range from "I know I have to look professional to be perceived as such," to "So you want me to dress like a Brooks Brothers model, right?" It is imperative that as minorities we dress the part. That is an integral part of professionalism. In the early 1980s, when I began my career with AT&T, I recall a new-hire sales training lecture with *Dress for Success* author John Molloy, where he instructed the class on proper business dress. It was a lesson I wished I had learned while interviewing during my senior year of college. I still remember the look of shock on the HR manager's face at Xerox when I showed up for my final round of interviews in a beige polyester suit with matching cowboy boots. I didn't get the job. Molloy's coaching, however, has remained with me, and I have never had to worry about self-imposed wardrobe malfunctions since.

"Dressing the part" is actually a significant part of executive presence, one of three important components that shape your brand:

- Executive presence
- Demonstrated competence
- Leadership quotient

Let's take a look at each.

Executive Presence

It is a fact that "you never get a second chance to make a first impression." This is an even greater proposition for the minority executive; from the moment you enter a boardroom, walk into an interview, or visit a client, there is something blatantly obvious—you look different. Unfortunately, in many of those encounters several thoughts come to mind: "Is she really qualified, or is this just a diversity hire?" In a moment of brutal honesty, I've had several white executives admit as much to me. However, one of the first things they also consider is, "Does she look the part?" While this is a function at all levels, when it comes to moving into senior management, the greater question is, "Does she have 'executive presence'?"

✦ *Denise's Story:*
How Changing Her Appearance Helped Her Career

Many years ago in Chicago, I worked with a sharp, intelligent, attractive woman named Denise at Ameritech. At the time, she was a high-potential middle manager moving up at the company. Years later, after both of us had left Ameritech, we reconnected at a professional networking event. She was now a director with her new employer and doing well, and I was an area vice president with Pitney Bowes. I was amazed that, given her talent and track record, she had not progressed further in the corporate ranks. During a conversation, she shared her frustration over how her female manager challenged her regarding her appearance at a recent business meeting.

Denise was very disturbed by her manager's assessment, but being familiar with Denise's style of form-fitting, sometimes revealing suits, I suggested that her attire might indeed be affecting her executive presence. It seemed as if she were drawing more attention to her physical form than was appropriate in a business setting. Denise took our conversation to heart, and indeed modified her wardrobe. It had not been totally inappropriate, but it hadn't fit with her new employer's culture. It has been a few years since we had this discussion, but Denise has earned two major promotions since that time. Furthermore, she has recently been recognized by *Diversity MBA* magazine as one of the Top 50/Under 50 minority executives in corporate America.

✦ Quincy's Story:
Not Dressed for Success

Quincy was a young, handsome, and very successful sales manager at Ameritech Cellular. He was also extremely frustrated. Quincy began as a sales rep whose work gained him a promotion to sales manager. In that role, he also performed well, continuing to exceed his quota. But Quincy's goal was to become a regional manager, a position he was consistently denied. Of course, his frustration grew as he continued to deliver strong sales results, but also continued to be passed over for promotion. He mistakenly thought that advancement would depend solely on his performance. In a regional management position, however, Quincy would be required to develop "C-suite" relationships (CEOs, COOs, CIOs, etc.) with clients, as well as represent Ameritech by speaking at conferences and trade shows. Unfortunately for Quincy, he did not present well at that level. His attire was often considered "loud and flashy" (he had a tendency to wear loud colored suits), and his delivery was considered more slick than seasoned. In the end, he was able to change his attire, but not his presence, and never rose to regional management level.

Key Questions on Executive Presence. Some of the executive presence questions my peers and I ask ourselves as we consider candidates for promotion:

1. How comfortable are we with this individual representing our company to senior-level executives from our key clients?
2. Is he "polished" enough to present in front of our executive leadership team or the company's board of directors?
3. Is he dynamic enough to engage an audience if he has to present information on corporate directives?

If the answer is no on more than one of these questions, that person may have an uphill battle for promotion to senior leadership.

Demonstrated Competence

Though executive presence can open the doors of opportunity, without competence those prospects can quickly dissipate. The equation is simple: Executive Presence − Competence = An Empty Suit. Webster defines *competence* as "the state or quality of being adequately or well qualified; ability" and "a specific range of skill, knowledge, or ability." But at the corporate level, and to contribute to the perception of the brand, competence has to be demonstrated.

Very often we tend to look at talent or ability from an "assumed" competence standpoint. For example, if you have an MBA in finance and a résumé that details specific job experience, we assume you have a degree of competence in the area of finance. But for this to be part of your brand and how you are perceived, you must demonstrate your skills and abilities consistently. What matters is how you distinguish yourself in an area—particularly since there will be several people in any given organization with the same knowledge base. While it is not essential or even possible for you to be completely competent in every area of business, it is critical that you demonstrate your abilities in those areas where you claim to add value.

If you are a minority executive, it is important that you seek opportunities to demonstrate your level of competence—particularly to those in senior-level positions. Sometimes the opportunity to serve on a project requires your expertise. Other times you may have an opportunity to move to an unpopular division that needs revamping. Ronald Williams's demonstrated ability to properly evaluate, restructure, and revive divisions in the health-care industry has contributed significantly to how he is viewed and what his competence is worth to an organization. It is equally important that those you lead are also confident in your abilities, as no one wants to take direction from someone they believe is incompetent.

Leadership Quotient

Certain skills are required of a senior leader beyond executive presence and demonstrated competence. These are the skills associated with the ability to direct and lead effectively. Though the first two brand components can be easily determined, the measuring of one's leadership quotient can be very subjective and sometimes difficult to gauge. Leadership quotient is the current and anticipated ability of an individual to effectively lead a major division, business unit, or total organization. It can, however, be defined by certain traits:

The ability to create "followership." Is this person capable of touching the hearts and minds of those in the organization, getting them to embrace her vision? Or does her style alienate employees, thus creating a disengaged workforce? Several examples demonstrate the correlation between a division or organizational leader's ability to empower and engage employees and the profitability of that department or organization. Two of my personal favorites are Lee Iacocca's transformation of Chrysler, and Lou Gerstner's ability to transform IBM from a mainframe-computer-driven organization into a service-based consulting company. It is not enough to be installed in a position of leadership. Successful leaders have to inspire drive, creativity, loyalty, and even leadership throughout the ranks.

The ability to work collaboratively with others. In this world of matrix organizations and cross-functional teams, very few leaders have the luxury of functioning as an independent unit. Today leaders are required to work across organizations strategically, coordinating with peers, company associates, and other department managers to get their jobs done and accomplish goals. To be successful across platforms and divisions requires being well networked across your company, as many successful collaborations are based on relationships that will help you understand the political structure of divisions outside of your department. How well an executive "plays in the sandbox" with others can have a tremendous impact on how effective he will be as a leader.

The ability to think strategically. The one trait that I have observed that most separates C-suite executives from other senior executives is their ability to think strategically. It is quite common to be able to create and achieve short-term goals based on the present market dynamics. It's a defining talent, however, to not only excel in the current market environment but also to anticipate the business environment of the future. The ability to predict the future, and prepare an organization to take advantage of what is yet to exist, makes an executive golden. History is littered with companies whose leaders couldn't see past the next quarterly earnings report. To move into senior leadership today, it is not good enough to be a strong tactical leader; one must develop and demonstrate the ability to think and act strategically.

COACHING TIPS

According to David Samuel, a leadership consultant and author of *Personal Branding Power: 65 Proven Strategies for Accelerated Career Growth*, there are four phases to professional branding:

Plan. During this crucial initial phase, assess your own portfolio of career assets (expertise, values, persona, and so on). Most important, define the value most in demand in your organization and industry. Your intent is to identify the best match between what's important to the market and what you can contribute in order to be perceived as valuable.

Develop. Take stock of your career values. What is truly important to you in your work? Perform a personal SWOT analysis to define your *strengths* and *weaknesses,* as well as the *opportunities* and *threats* associated with your career. During this phase you are also identifying and closing important skill gaps. Your intent is to determine how to strengthen your existing expertise and develop new expertise that creates the best professional value for the organization.

Promote. During this phase you are clarifying your personal value proposition, and promoting that value proposition through the most effective "branding channels" in your organization and industry. Define a crisp personal value proposition statement that articulates it well. Construct an electronic portfolio of "product information," including your résumé, corporate bio/head shot, case studies, personal FAQs, and even a personal "brochure." Build the kit around your personal value proposition. A simple but very powerful example of how such a kit can be displayed and available online can be found at www.leanforwardandgo.com/cda.html. Feel free to adapt that model to your own situation. Your intent is to proactively manage your personal brand to attract the best career growth opportunities.

Connect. During this phase you are connecting your value proposition to the organization through the strong advocacy relationships that you are developing. Your intent is to build and use your professional network to further accelerate the impact of your personal brand. You can do this through several vehicles such as LinkedIn, Ziggs, and Navagility. In addition to the profiling tools mentioned, it is important to use digital branding platforms such as e-mail, blogs, and even your own Web site to promote your value proposition. The secret to attracting opportunities is to connect your value proposition to Google and other search engines. Simply embed high-impact keywords into your digital branding platforms and documents. Those keywords attract the search engines, and the search engines will pave the path for hiring managers and clients to find you! Samuel believes there are several ways to further your "campaign":

- **Create strong advocates.** Develop and nurture relationships with others who will advocate for you, both formally and informally. Choose your advocates carefully and strategically. The best advocates are those who are committed to your success and have influence in the organization, so that their advocacy is meaningful.

- **Give visibility to your thought leadership.** Actively seek opportunities to publish your ideas (industry articles, blogs, special reports) and present them in public speaking situations. These can be company meetings or industry conferences. Nervous about public speaking? Get over it! Take a Toastmasters course. Public speaking is an essential personal branding tool.

- **Demonstrate industry leadership.** Increase your participation in the right industry and professional associations. Select strategically important committees, and continually make meaningful contributions with your knowledge and insight.

3

Be Visible

You Can't Get Ahead
If No One Knows Who You Are

Previously, we discussed the importance of perception and the idea of personal branding. On the surface, it would seem that having a personal brand and a positive image would be all that is required to be considered for promotions and key assignments. The truth is, while it is extremely important to have these things, they mean very little if you lack visibility with the power brokers within your organization. To make matters more challenging, getting that visibility can be easier said than done.

The concept of being visible is not rocket science. In fact, it may even sound simplistic. However, over the years I have observed far too many minority careers hit a standstill because the individual missed the following:

- Didn't understand the value of visibility;
- Didn't take advantage of opportunities to be more visible; or

- Didn't present himself positively during "key visibility encounters."

Having had the good fortune to have served as a mentor to many up-and-coming professionals, I was able to get a better understanding of why these otherwise intelligent, high-performing individuals were seemingly missing the boat as regards visibility. More often than not, there were certain hidden biases, some even cultural, that hindered them from even pursuing opportunities for visibility:

If I am doing great work, I shouldn't *have* to work on being visible. The fallacy here is that it is the responsibility of others to notice your work, and also their responsibility to reward and recognize you. This is not proactive at all, and puts others in the driver's seat of your career.

The more visible I am, the more I will stand out. Those who think this way are afraid to take the risk of being visible. While visibility can be a double-edged sword, if you are not willing to take the risk of standing out, you will also never reap the rewards it can bring. Sayings like "The nail that sticks up the highest is the first to get hit by the hammer" have caused many minorities to avoid making themselves more visible.

Making myself visible is akin to bragging, and is not polite. While bragging is not polite, the intent of the braggart is to tell the world how wonderful he is. Visibility is more an act of letting others see who you are, and what you bring to the table. From there, they can draw their own conclusions. Furthermore, in certain minority cultures it is not acceptable to "brag" or "boast" about accomplishments. I can remember personally as a child being scolded by my elders for telling my cousins about my great report card. The fear was twofold: first, that I would somehow get a "big head," and second, that making public my grades might make my cousins feel bad if their own grades were not as good. Many minorities take this thinking into adulthood, and as a result, they don't take advantage of opportunities to be more visible.

To be visible requires extra work or extra effort and is not worth it. The honest truth is, it does require extra effort to be visible. You may have to volunteer for extra work, you may have to create and deliver an additional presentation. You may even have to attend an event that you may not care for, or learn a sport (golf) that you do not know how to play. But this effort will only be worthless if the product you represent (you) has no value.

THE ONLY ONE IN THE ROOM? MAKE VISIBILITY WORK FOR YOU!

As a minority professional, there will be many times you will find yourself the only one in the room. For some, this can be an intimidating and frightening experience. You feel as if your every move is watched, your every word dissected under a microscope, and that basically everyone else in the room is against you. Others look at this and consider it an opportunity. Ken Chenault, chairman and CEO of American Express, believes that rather than be intimidated in such environments, you should look at them as an opportunity to increase your visibility. In her book *Take a Lesson: Today's Black Achievers on How They Made It and What They Learned*, Caroline V.

Clarke highlights Chenault's theory on being the "only one in the room." Says Chenault, "Recognize that being one of the only blacks, whether in a classroom, in a department, on a work team, in an organization, or just in a meeting—*automatically* makes you very visible. Use this to help yourself. Look at it as an opportunity, and leverage that opportunity by making a visible *contribution*." Put in this perspective, being the only one in the room can actually work to your benefit, as it gives you instant visibility and, with that, the chance to stand out.

✦ *Manny's (Almost) Missed Opportunity*

A few years ago, while I was an area VP for Pitney Bowes, I invited several of my Latino managers and directors to attend the awards dinner at the annual National Society of Hispanic MBAs in Anaheim, California. The event was on a Saturday evening, and Pitney was receiving the Brillante Award from the organization. In total, I invited four young Latino professionals to attend, all from the southern California area. On the day of the event, one by one they all called my manager of diversity to inform her they had to cancel. Disappointed, I had her contact them all to share how unfortunate it was they could not attend.

However, one gentleman, Manny, called back to say he could attend for a portion of the evening. I arranged for Manny to sit next to me at dinner, and we had a terrific conversation. He even admitted that his real reason for canceling earlier was that he had a "hot date" he didn't want to miss. I assured him that she would still be there, and he left to enjoy the rest of his evening. What he didn't know was that I was planning an organizational change in the next few months and wanted to get to know him better, as he was a candidate for a promotion to director. Because he made the wise "investment" of attending that dinner, he was later promoted to director in Los Angeles and has since been given even greater responsibility by my successor.

Being visible comes across to others as "sucking up," and is not honorable. No one likes to be viewed as a "suck-up." In fact, it is a characteristic that is not only resented by peers but also frowned upon by management. It can disrupt teamwork and create animosity. The perception that you are trying to develop relationships with those higher in the organization can make some distrust you and question your motives. Just as in grade school no one liked the teacher's pet, you must be careful that when you make yourself visible to senior leadership, you do so tactfully. If not, you could develop animosity among your peers.

At first glance, these all sound like logical reasons to ignore opportunities for visibility. However, they are based on faulty reasoning that could work to your disadvantage in your effort to get to the senior level. Additionally, anyone who does not understand the importance of visibility most likely does not understand the importance of succession planning!

WHY VISIBILITY MATTERS: SUCCESSION PLANNING

In almost every Fortune 1000 company there is an event that takes place at least annually that has the greatest impact on future promotions and leadership opportunities. It typically involves every senior-level officer, including the CEO, and for some positions, it will even involve the board of directors. It is also the one event where your performance, personal branding, mentor/sponsor relationships, and visibility count the most. That event is the succession planning meeting.

At its most simplistic level, this meeting (or series of meetings) is reminiscent of the NFL draft. Typically, starting at the highest level of the organization down to the first-level manager, all the players are identified, discussed, and rated. The ratings can take many forms, but typically the first round of ratings involves ranking the players by peer group (manager, director, VP), as either an A, B, C, or D level player. If you are rated an A player, you are typically in the top 15 percent of your peer group. As a B player, you are in the next 25 percent based on performance, and if you are a C player you most likely are considered "average"; this category accounts for approximately 50 percent of the population. The remaining 10 percent are labeled "D" players and are usually slated for disciplinary action, demotion, or dismissal; thus, not much time is spent on these individuals.

While you might assume that these ratings are based solely on job performance, in reality there are other factors that make up these ratings. These can include the following:

- Performance rating for current and previous year.
- Performance against company-identified leadership competencies.
- Potential for promotion.

Let's take a closer look at why these are important.

Performance rating for current and previous year. If you are to even begin to be considered for promotional opportunities, it is imperative that you be performing at a high level in your current role. I am often amazed at those individuals who expect to be considered for additional responsibility and haven't demonstrated the ability to excel in their current role. The first brick on the road to success—and promotion—is to exceed expectations in your existing role. Additionally, because senior leaders value consistency in performance, in many cases you will also be evaluated based on performance in a prior role or in the previous year. We're all familiar with the "one-hit wonder," the person who has a great year and is never heard from again. In the hit music world we see this all the time—think Billy Ray Cyrus's "Achy Breaky Heart," Tag Team's "Whoomp! (There It Is)," or Bobby McFerrin's "Don't Worry, Be Happy." Likewise, in the corporate world no one likes to bank on a player who has only one good year under his belt. As a result, a premium is placed on performance over time, and it is important to have a body of work that demonstrates your ability to deliver results year in, year-out.

Performance against company leadership competencies. While performance against set goals or objectives in a given role is the first brick on the road to senior leadership, it is only the ticket you must have to get into the game. At the first- and even second-level management layer, basic job performance can get you promoted; but to make the leap into senior management requires that you demonstrate your ability to meet the leadership competencies identified by your company. While they are often published, very often these competencies are shared only among HR and senior-level leadership and are not common knowledge, least of all to minorities.

Typically, these competencies revolve around:

- **Strategic visioning.** Looks outside-in for external perspectives, trends, and solutions; discerns global and competitive trends; clearly articulates a vision and direction; demonstrates adaptability and flexibility, recognizing that change is necessary.

- **Results-driven management.** Understands financial statements and other key drivers and metrics for business success; makes decisions with an appropriate sense of urgency; is inclusive but not consensus-driven; influences others to gain support to get things done.
- **Leading for growth.** Takes intelligent risks for growth; understands and anticipates customer needs and perspectives; looks for creative solutions to both simple and complex problems; accepts that for a company to survive it must grow; looks for growth opportunities with out-of-the-box thinking.
- **Inspiring and motivating talent.** Committed to attracting and selecting high-performing people of diverse cultures; sets challenging but achievable objectives and allows people the latitude to achieve; provides regular direct feedback; motivates in a positive manner.

Unfortunately, many minorities are either unaware of or not developed in many of these competencies, and can thus fall short when it comes to competing for promotion.

✦ Marco's Challenge

A year ago I had the pleasure of working with Marco, a regional sales manager on the West Coast who worked for a high-tech manufacturing company. Marco had worked for the company roughly seven years; he was their top sales rep, and eventually got promoted to sales manager and later regional sales manager. He was sharp, good in front of clients, and above all, always exceeded his sales targets. However, Marco could never get promoted to the vice president level. Twice before he had interviewed, and both times he lost out to a peer who seemingly had lesser sales results than Marco. To his credit, both times Marco asked for feedback and was told that while his results were great, his style was not what the company was looking for in the VP role. After I agreed to mentor Marco, several things became obvious:

1. He didn't realize he was being evaluated on more than just his sales results.
2. While he did deliver sales results, and clients loved him, he was considered a pain by those who worked with him internally.
3. He wasn't doing a great job at "developing" his people. He either sold for them or sold with them, never teaching them how to sell for themselves.

After sharing my observations with Marco in a tough-love mentoring session in which I basically informed him that his bull-in-a-china-shop behavior was not only isolating him from his coworkers but hindering his ability to get promoted, I encouraged him to have a 360-degree evaluation performed on him based upon his company's leadership competencies. Needless to say, the results were eye-opening. He was now able to see himself as others saw him and understand how he ranked against what his company was looking for in a senior leader. He has since begun to modify his behavior and be more collaborative with peers, and more development-oriented with his people.

POTENTIAL FOR PROMOTION

One of the key outcomes of the succession planning process is to identify candidates for promotion to greater responsibility. In many cases, these individuals get labeled according to the time frame of their expected promotion. Typically, they are labeled in one of the following ways:

Ready now. These players have consistent performance, have demonstrated many of the company's leadership competencies, and are ready for their next assignment.

Ready in a year. These individuals have demonstrated consistent performance, but may need another year to grow in one or more areas in the leadership competency model.

Ready in two to three years. These individuals exhibit excellent performance and may have some of the leadership competencies, but need to show consistent performance over time. These people typically make up the "feeder pool" and are the next generation of "ready in a year" and "ready now" candidates.

Not ready. These individuals are meeting expectations in their current role, and may even demonstrate one or two of the leadership competencies. However, they are considered either "average" workers or players who have gone as far as they can go in the organization.

WHY VISIBILITY MATTERS: HOW IS YOUR RANKING DETERMINED?

Earlier in this chapter I stated that the succession planning process is the one event where your performance, personal branding, mentor/sponsor relationships, and visibility count the most. Why do I make this statement? Because of *how* your ranking is determined in these meetings. In almost every situation I am aware of, there is discussion in a group environment as to how each player gets ranked. Typically, your immediate manager will offer a recommendation, share some of your key attributes, and open the floor for feedback. At this point, others in the room will offer their opinion or share past experiences or interactions with the individual. After final discussions, the persons ranked will either remain where their manager suggested, or go up or down based upon outside feedback. This is where visibility counts the most!

✦ A Personal Experience with Visibility

If you want to get to the senior level of leadership, you must become more visible in your company or organization, because (as the subtitle to this chapter says) you can't get ahead if nobody knows who you are. I learned this lesson firsthand three years ago from my boss at Pitney Bowes. I joined the company as a senior VP, so I had a fairly high-level job in one of the company's largest business units. At my first annual review, however, my boss said, "I have good news and bad news. The good news is, you're a great performer in our business unit. The bad news is, at this year's succession planning meeting, no one outside our business unit knew you. You need to understand that for you to get promoted, either in my organization or outside my organization, you have to be known by other people." My boss then helped me improve my visibility company-wide, by providing me access to board members and key executive leadership council members. He also allowed me to make presentations to these people on behalf of the business unit (instead of presenting himself). And he recommended me for membership on the company-wide transformation committee, made up of board members and executive leadership, to further raise my profile. And because of that increased visibility, in the course of a year I was promoted to the job I now have, which is president of all U.S. operations for Pitney Bowes Management Services.

In this case, I was fortunate—not to diminish my qualifications for this job, but if my boss hadn't recognized that I needed to be known by more people, and if my boss hadn't helped me, I might not have been promoted, or at least not as soon.

WHY VISIBILITY MATTERS: "WHO'S WEARING YOUR T-SHIRT?"

Recently, I invited David Samuel, one of the leading authorities on personal branding, to facilitate a diversity development program for high-potential minority professionals at Pitney Bowes. At one point during his lecture, he showed a photo of a couple in which the man is wearing a T-shirt that proclaims boldly, "Damn, I'm Good." He then went on to explain that this image always elicits a strong negative reaction from observers, who frequently note how arrogant that message appears. He then reminded the class that while it's important to be confident, you can take it too far.

He then presented the same photo with the woman wearing a T-shirt that stated, "Damn, He's Good" in reference to her partner. As you might have guessed, this picture painted the man in a much different light. Because someone else was wearing his T-shirt, he had instant credibility and did not have to proclaim how wonderful he was. Furthermore, even when he was not around, he was still visible because she was wearing his T-shirt.

The question is, who is wearing *your* T-shirt? When the succession planning meetings take place, is there someone in the room with a T-shirt proclaiming how great you are? When names are being kicked around on a golf course as to who might be a great candidate to head up the new acquisition, is someone in that foursome wearing your T-shirt? At the end of the day, you need to make sure that there are as many people as possible wearing your T-shirt. Invisible people don't get promoted!

COACHING TIPS

As indicated throughout this chapter, visibility, if properly managed, can be a tremendous asset to the minority professional. Making sure that the *right* people know the *right* things about you and your career goals and ambitions can be the difference between being a HiPo (high-potential) and a PoPo (passed over and pissed off) player. While in the past, you may not have felt the need or importance to focus on being visible, the following are some suggestions to help you increase your visibility and enhance your ability to be promoted.

Don't look for gold stars at work. Many of us can recall as kids getting a gold star on our paper or report cards from our elementary school teacher. In those days, you did your work, the teacher noticed how well you did, and you were rewarded. If it took getting a 95 percent grade to get a star, *everyone* who earned a 95 percent or higher got a star. The trend continued in college, when professors would often grade on a curve, but in the end, you were graded and rewarded in the same manner as your fellow classmates. However, in the real world of business, never assume that just because you are doing great work, you will get noticed and rewarded. Your boss is not like your teacher, who gives out gold stars to everyone who performs well. If you are waiting for others to notice how well you are doing and offer you a fat raise and a big promotion, you will likely be waiting for some time. Remember, it's up to you to make sure that your accomplishments, successes, and aspirations are visible to those who have influence over your career.

Meet with your boss to review your performance regularly. One of the biggest mistakes I see young minority professionals make is not documenting the expectations the company has set for them, and then not meeting with management on a regular basis to update them on their progress and to make sure they are on target. There is nothing worse than receiving your annual performance appraisal and being in shock that you and your boss don't see eye to eye on your performance. By meeting with your boss at least quarterly, you will be able to measure your accomplishments against your goals, and if there are any areas that need improvement, you will have time to address them before it's too late. Conversely, if you have exceeded expectations or performed tasks worthy of recognition, you will have the ability to inform management right then, rather than waiting until the end of the work year.

Attempt to meet with your boss's boss at least once a year. In an ideal world, your immediate manager should be your biggest supporter. She should be the one who is "wearing your T-shirt" in plain view of the organization, letting them know how well you are doing, and looking for opportunities to develop you and advance your career. The reality is, in many cases your boss may not be able or willing to do this. Given the demands placed on managers today, she may actually not have the time or opportunity to sing your praises. Or you could be more valuable to her in the role you are already in, and she may not want to risk losing you to a promotion. In either case, you'll need to toot your own horn. I advise that at least once a year you request a "skip-level" meeting with your boss's boss. I suggest that *prior* to this meeting, it is wise to make it clear that you just want to get a better understanding of the company's goals and expectations, and also receive from the "big boss" his vision for the department or business unit. However, *during* the meeting, once the leader shares his vision and the *company's* goals, take the liberty to tell the senior leader about your accomplishments in support of these goals, and other ways you feel you can add value. You will be amazed by how such a simple meeting can enhance your visibility. *Warning:* Your immediate manager may not be comfortable with this meeting, so make certain to inform her ahead of time, and after the meeting, tell her what you discussed in it.

Find ways to meet formally or informally with other senior leaders. Because of succession planning, it's important that you are visible to as many senior leaders as possible. Ideally, you can apply the same logic outlined above for the meeting with your boss's boss to meeting with other senior leaders in your company: wanting to know more about their business unit or function, and how you may be able to add value. However, your end goal is to share your accomplishments with these leaders and leave them with a good impression of you. If for some reason it is not possible to arrange such a meeting formally, look for ways to do so informally—perhaps sitting next to such a leader at a company function, or playing in his foursome at the next company outing. No matter how and where you have to get their attention, make sure you look for opportunities to increase your visibility with these power brokers. In my career I have even gone as far as to volunteer to pick up a senior leader at the airport when he arrived in town. It cost me a few dollars in gasoline, but it bought me, on average, an hour of face time with a senior leader. You never know when an opportunity may come up in their department or division.

Consider volunteering for company-wide initiatives. Working on the company holiday party or annual employee giving campaign may not sound like something you want to sign up for, but there is a side benefit in doing so. Typically, since these initiatives cross multiple company departments and divisions, they often require interfacing with the leaders of those departments and divisions. It is during these meetings that you get to showcase your creativity, project management ability, and interpersonal skills.

Attend key company events. While some of these events can be a drain on your personal time, consider attending those company events that will give you access and visibility to key senior leaders. It could be the retirement party for a beloved associate, the holiday event at your boss's home, or the annual company golf outing. If key senior leaders are in attendance, it could be your chance to make a good impression.

4

Know When to Move Over and When to Get Out

Taking a Lateral Job versus Leaving Your Company

The number one concern frequently expressed by minority managers is, "I'm frustrated where I am; things aren't happening for me here. My company has only offered me a lateral move. Should I hang in there and hope for the best, and maybe I'll be promoted in the future, or is the writing on the wall, telling me that I'll never get promoted, so I should just move on to another company?"

Knowing when to take a lateral job offer and when to turn it down and move to another company is a difficult decision. In this chapter, we will consider examples of people who have made the right decision—and some who made the wrong one. These will help you understand how to make the right decision for *you*, based on your specific goals. Let's start by looking at some real-life situations that have happened to a few of my colleagues and mentees.

MOVE LATERALLY WHEN YOU NEED
TO BROADEN YOUR EXPERIENCE

✦ *Kyle's Story*

Kyle was a young salesperson at Cingular who sought my advice because he had been turned down for a promotion. Instead of his dream job, his company offered him a staff job where he would manage dealers who sold cell phones. Kyle was disappointed that he did not get the promotion, and questioned taking this lateral move. Kyle's ultimate goal was to become a general manager. Because his experience was limited to sales, it was important for him to be in a position where he would gain experience in managing dealers. After much discussion and weighing of options, Kyle took the job. After two years, Kyle was promoted as general manager of the northern Ohio market, which would not have happened had he not been given the chance to manage.

This was a clear case of a *lateral* move being the *right* move. Kyle was able to put his long-range goals *first* and forgo immediate gratification. A lateral move can actually be the *best* way to climb the career ladder in the long run—even though it may seem like you are taking a side step instead of a move up—because it helps you *broaden* your experience. Admittedly, that's not always easy, as we will see in this next case.

✦ *Carl's Story*

Carl was the director of sales at a medical equipment company. He was offered a lateral position in his company holding the same job title, but for Latin America instead of the United States. Initially, he did not want to accept the position because of the relocation. It was not as though he had to move to Latin America, but he would have to relocate to Florida. However, Carl was true to his West Coast roots and did not want to move. Carl needed to consider the advantages of this opportunity as it related to achieving his long-range goals. For him to be considered for further promotions, international exposure and experience would be very important, so Carl accepted the job and moved to Florida. After two years of managing the Latin American operations, Carl was promoted to senior vice president of sales for the Canadian division of the company. That would never have happened if he had not had the experience of managing Latin America. That lateral move broadened his background and expertise considerably, allowing him to move up substantially in the organization later down the road.

DON'T MOVE JUST FOR A BETTER TITLE OR MORE MONEY

At the risk of sounding contradictory, understand that a promotion may not always be the best move for your career. When you are offered any position, you must consider all the factors. In doing so, you may conclude that some factors may actually detract from your ability to succeed in a higher-level position. Let's consider another case.

✦ Ernie's Story

Ernie was a first-level manager in an Atlanta-based communications company. He did his job well, but he really wanted a promotion to branch manager. The company kept putting him off, and finally he threatened legal action. To avoid a lawsuit, the company acquiesced and promoted Ernie to branch manager in a small town in Indiana. Ernie was advised by colleagues to visit the town and get a taste for its culture and environment. This advice was offered because Ernie was an African American, and the client base might not be conducive to African American leadership. Ernie made the decision to accept the position, without following the advice, and lasted one year. The short tenure was due not to lack of ability but to environmental factors. In fact, Ernie was so unsuccessful at running the small-town branch that he was on the verge of being fired. Ultimately, Ernie was demoted and moved to another city.

If this manager had only waited for the *right* region to come along, he might have been more successful. Ernie is lucky to have a job today. Here was a talented, skilled manager who wanted the "branch manager" title so desperately that he risked jeopardizing his whole career with this company. Essentially, he took two steps forward and three steps back. If only he had waited for a more favorable situation.

Do not make the same mistake Ernie did. Do not allow yourself to be seduced by a better job title or increased compensation. Instead, keep in mind your *long-range* goals, and how this potential new position will impact your goals. If this position will not propel you closer to your goal, this may not be the best opportunity for you at this time. *Be patient,* and keep in mind your *ultimate* career goals.

DON'T LEAVE A COMPANY WHERE YOU *CAN* MOVE UP FOR A "BETTER JOB" AT A COMPANY WHERE YOU *CAN'T* MOVE UP

Weighing options for promotion within your current company versus a new position with a new company is another challenge to consider. Many people think this is a no-brainer: if you are offered a better job at a better company, you should take it, right? Most people have heard comments such as, "The only way to move up and make more money is to move around," right? Wrong! Or at least, not always. Just because our current work culture no longer necessarily rewards those who have rendered forty-five years of service to the same company, that does not mean there are not rewarding opportunities available with your current company. Think long and hard before you walk away from your current employer: you may not be able to return, and the company you're working for now just might prove to be the *best* company with *the most potential for your career* in the long run.

✦ *Nathan's Story*

A good example is a recent conversation I had with a younger executive I have known for a few years. Nathan had worked for many years for a huge company. This company was a leader in its industry, and may very well have been number one. Nathan reached the level of director, but he had aspirations of becoming a vice president. So he left the industry leader to go to a much smaller, privately held company. Why? Because he was offered the title of vice president. Nathan worked for the new company for two years, and was very instrumental in helping them to double their sales. Unfortunately, they only wanted to acquire Nathan's knowledge and experience. After obtaining what they wanted, they kept the knowledge, and basically had no other need for Nathan.

Nathan got his vice president title, and a few extra dollars, but now he is very frustrated. Being the only minority in leadership at this small company, he quickly found out that a few select people hold power, and he would never be able to achieve his true goals there. Sadly, he cannot return to his former organization because the company culture does not allow for it. When he made a written request to his former company, asking to be considered for another job, he was declined. Although Nathan is still employed with the smaller company, he is miserable.

Fortunately, every corporate culture is different. The company I work for, Pitney Bowes, is the exact opposite of the company just described. Pitney Bowes is probably the exception to the rule, however; it is rare to find a company where you can leave and return at your convenience. Let's consider Susan's situation.

✦ Susan's Story

Susan was a senior sales executive who left her job for a new position with another company. Her new job did not work out, and she returned to her previous employer at a higher level than when she left. Her new position was vice president of sales. Her former employer recognized that she had not been working to her maximum ability when she left, so they promoted her when she returned. But the culture here is different. You have to know what the culture is in the company you are working for. Again, in some companies, once you leave, returning is often tough and sometimes impossible.

SMALL VERSUS LARGE CORPORATIONS

If you are considering moving to a smaller company because you think you will have more opportunity to be "a big fish in a small pond," keep in mind that larger companies do have certain benefits because of their size. Going back to Nathan's story, his previous company was very hierarchical, and Nathan did not realize the benefits of that until *after* he left. Transitioning to a smaller company proved to be a step in the wrong direction. At the smaller company, power was more tightly held, and little recourse is available to battle that. By contrast, if issues of discrimination or any other problem from a human resource perspective had arisen in his former company, it could have been easily dealt with. Why? Because it was a large public company, and it had concerns about being sued and preventing litigation. Thus Nathan's former company was actually a *better* company, because it ensured that people were promoted fairly to avoid legal action on the part of the employee. Be aware that larger companies take those kinds of issues seriously, whereas smaller companies may often react to complaints from employees with an attitude of "You don't like it here? So what, go ahead and leave."

On the other hand, smaller companies are sometimes better, depending on your personality and what you are looking for. And this may have nothing to do with the fact that you are a minority. Other issues affect your comfort level at an organization. Let's take a look at our next case.

✦ Lorraine's Story

Lorraine was frustrated with the bureaucracy at the large software company where she worked. She felt her ideas were never taken seriously or considered by senior leadership. The company had an industry-leading product and did not really want to make any changes to it. Therefore, most ideas submitted, including Lorraine's, were shelved. Lorraine left the company and joined a smaller start-up software company that had significant venture capital funding. She is more fulfilled there, and several of her ideas have been implemented.

In this case, the color of Lorraine's skin had nothing to do with the job. Instead, it was the size of the company that determined her comfort level. Race may have played a small factor in her decision. Initially, she may have rejected the thought of going to a smaller company, because these are often not as friendly to minorities as larger companies are. She may have thought, "Oh, no, I'm going to be the token black woman there." But after her interview, she saw that her fears were unfounded. The hiring manager talked about how the company embraced new ideas and was looking for creative, entrepreneurial people to be a part of their team. While touring the company, she noticed a foosball table in the cafeteria, and saw that the employees were dressed very casually. She felt good vibes, unlike the almost militaristic environment of the company she had been working for. She said, "It felt like Silicon Valley had left California and moved to Chicago." It is important to find out how you will fit into a new company. Do not consider only the issue of being a minority; consider your entire personality and background. Lorraine fit in better with a smaller company.

Finally, another factor to keep in mind is location. Very often it can be to your advantage to work at the corporate headquarters. In fact, as the story below suggests, it can even accelerate your career. Jordan was another very young manager who expressed his frustration with his job. His concern was that he had been with his company two years, and nothing had happened. He was not moving fast enough, for him. But two years is not a long time at a lot of companies, and you have to consider the company you are working for. In this case, Jordan was working for FedEx, and Jordan needed to be reminded of just how great a company FedEx is. Moreover, he worked at the headquarters in Memphis, Tennessee, which is the ideal place for him to be if he wanted to move up to senior management. The advice given to Jordan was to be patient, and after eighteen months, he received the promotion he desired.

In some cases, however, you can wait too long. Gerri is another young manager I know who worked for a company where she felt she was not a good fit because it was a very male-dominated culture. No women—or people of color—had positions higher than the director level. Even after being with her company for ten years, Gerri was never given the opportunity to interview for certain positions. In this case, it was wise for Gerri to move on because it seemed she had reached the end of the road in this organization. Gerri had certainly worked there a long time, and she had looked at the right factors to see what her chances for advancement were. She contacted an executive search firm specializing in minority placements, and she was placed in a great job with a 25 percent increase in salary at one of the largest banks in America.

CREATE A BLUEPRINT FOR YOUR CAREER

The best way to make decisions about your career is to create a blueprint that will guide you to your ultimate destination. The key to achieving your goals is to always keep the end in mind. Most high-level professionals will tell you to simply look out three to five years down the road, but I take a different approach. In addition to looking at where you want to be three to five years from now, it is important to also look out to the end of your career and ask yourself, "Okay, where do I want to end up? What do I want to be? What do I want that last job to look like for me?" Then work backward to see what kinds of experiences, what types of jobs, and what else is needed to prepare you for the job that will lead to your ultimate goal. Continue doing the same exercise for each job on your career ladder, until you work your way back to where you are right now. Essentially, you should be making a strategic plan for your career.

This can be a bit difficult, especially for younger professionals who are just starting out and think, "I am only twenty-five years old; how do I know where I want to be or what I want to be doing when I am sixty-five?" Even people who knew what they wanted from a very young age—like kids who just knew they wanted to be a doctor when they grew up—rarely knew that they wanted to be the head of a hospital, or the surgeon general of the United States! Still, even when it is tough to do, creating a blueprint is really beneficial to your career. Moreover, your blueprint is not something you create just once; you should create a new one as you advance in your career, because for most people, your goals will change.

The large majority of people reading this book are probably *not* just starting out in their careers. Instead, you have more than likely established a track of some sort, and probably have a good picture of what you want the end of your career to look like. So let's examine my personal blueprint, which can serve as a template to help you achieve more challenging and creative goals within the different stages of your career and help *you* think about how *you* can create, revise, and revisit your own blueprint as you climb your own career ladder.

Creating Your First Blueprint—Get Started in the Right Direction

I created my first career blueprint over twenty years ago, in 1987. I was employed, but I was also in graduate school earning an MBA. The first thing I said to myself was, "I want to end my career as a senior vice president of sales in a Fortune 1000 company." That was the first brick laid in creating my career blueprint. Based on my background and the knowledge that I had at the time, I then considered what industry I wanted to work in, and chose information technology. And not only did I want to work in the information technology industry, I wanted to work for one of the *top* information technology companies, and at that time, IBM was number one. I cast my net with the top three companies, and landed a position with IBM.

To relocate or not to relocate. The other factor that was important to me was geographic location. I had to determine whether I wanted to confine myself to one particular region of the country, or if I would be willing to work in any part of the country. Taking this into consideration could limit my choices of jobs to take. I had to make a decision: Would I be willing to move from coast to coast? If the right opportunity came up, was I willing to relocate and uproot my family? And so, geography caused me to rethink my career decisions. As such, my rationale was that I would move up the career ladder more quickly if I was willing to relocate. It must be understood that if you are not willing to relocate, you have limited your opportunity to get promoted. It may still happen, but it will take longer in most cases.

That was how I created my first career blueprint. My ultimate goal at that time was to become senior vice president of sales for a Fortune 1000 company in the technology industry, anywhere in the United States. From that goal, I worked backward to see how I could best achieve that goal. Because my focus was on sales, I understood the importance of assuming increasingly larger areas of responsibility: I needed to move from a sales representative, to a sales manager, to a sales director, and that was the path I charted in my first career blueprint.

As you can see, developing a blueprint for your career requires a lot of consideration, and I did not create this all on my own; I had input from others. I bounced ideas off my mentors, who gave me guidance and coaching. These were typically senior executives I had known through the years, primarily (though not exclusively) African American. They were either people I had worked for or people in my community whom I had grown up with. They were people I admired and respected. They were not people who currently worked for the company I was working for, but they were friendly, professional colleagues from previous jobs. And they provided insight and input to my blueprint during informal conversations, usually over breakfast. One of my mentors liked to meet at the barbershop, so we would talk there. The key is to be flexible, and meet where it is convenient for your mentors. When I requested a meeting with my mentors, I would always make sure they knew our meeting would have an agenda. It was important to me that they understood I was seeking advice on a particular issue, and this would not be just a social visit. I would let them know I wanted their advice on ideas I was contemplating, when they had time, at their convenience. Those meetings and their input helped me enormously to develop my career blueprint.

That is how I still do things today. Obviously, as my career has progressed, I have updated my first blueprint several times since I created it twenty years ago. Once I achieved my goal of being senior vice president of sales, I realized that I wanted to be an even bigger player, which led me to create a new blueprint for the next level in my career.

So, what are the lessons learned here? First, you not only need to *create* a blueprint for your career; you also need to *update* it every few years or so, to make sure you are still aiming high and making the progress that will lead you to greater heights. It is great to achieve the goals you have set for yourself, but you will be even happier and more successful if you continue to set *new* goals to do better (and more!) in your career and in your life overall. You need to continue to expand your vision of yourself.

Second, when you are creating your blueprint, it is vital to take the time to actually sit down and put it in writing. Anyone who knows anything about setting and achieving goals will tell you that it is critical to *write it down!* A plan and goals are just that—not tangible. It is harder to make them real if you do not commit them to writing. On the other hand, you are not setting them in stone to the point where you cannot alter them if necessary. You are simply jotting down notes to keep you on track.

Creating Your Second Blueprint— Broaden Your Experience

About three to five years after creating my first blueprint, I was about thirty years old, and I thought, "Sales is great, and I make good money, but I think I have a lot more to offer than just selling."

That thought caused me to change my blueprint. I realized I had to seek the opportunity if I wanted to be a general manager or president of a company. I recognized that I needed to have experience in finance, strategic planning, and understanding customer service. So that led me to a different track in my career.

While working at Ameritech, I decided to move from sales to overseeing customer service. I was able to do that by basically leveraging my background in sales. Fortunately, I did this during a time when many companies (and especially phone companies) were looking to make their customer service representatives more sales-oriented. For example, when a customer called to cancel her phone service, or to get another line added, the customer service representative would try to sell the customer another service. For instance, the representative would ask, "Do you want call waiting; do you want long distance?" So I was at the right time and right place to add customer service to my sales background. My company basically said to me, "Okay, we will teach you customer service, but you have a great background in being a sales leader. So why don't you turn our customer service representatives into a sales organization?"

This was actually a lateral move in one sense, because the title was a lateral title change. It was also a step down for me financially because in sales, I typically earned bonuses and commissions based on what I sold, and this new job was not commissionable. While I made less money that year, the lateral move prepared me for something greater. That was a trade-off I decided to make. I went from the sales director at the company to the customer service director of the same company, and I did that for about eighteen months. Then I earned a promotion to general manager of sales and customer service. That had not been discussed at the time I took the customer service job— but it was on my radar, even if it was not on anyone else's!

What is the lesson here? You need to consider what the best move is for *you* at various points in your career: What changes should *you* be making in your career to achieve your ultimate goals? In other words, do not let your current success limit you. Many companies will want you to stay where you are if you are doing a great job for the company, but you need to consider *your* personal goals first, before the goals of your company. If you are successful at the level you are currently working at, that is terrific. But every few years, you should think whether you will really be happy doing this for the rest of your career, or if you would like to climb higher on the corporate ladder and accomplish even more. If you do want that, then assess your skills and see what you need to broaden your experience to get to the next level of your career. I will talk more about how to do that later in this chapter.

Creating Your Third Blueprint— Reach the Highest Levels of Management

After overseeing both sales and customer service at Ameritech, I got a taste of general management life. I was fortunate that the company recognized my ability. My bosses assigned more and more responsibility and other functional areas to me, thus broadening my experience even further. Eventually, you name it and it all fell under my jurisdiction. Then I began to realize, "Okay, there is a possibility I could become a CEO." Part of that came from being on different task forces. The first time I really thought seriously that I might have a chance to be a CEO was around 1997, ten years ago, when I was about thirty-seven. So I revisited my blueprint once again.

Thinking in terms of CEO, I knew I definitely needed to develop a lot more financial profit-and-loss responsibility. I needed to position myself where I had a large number of people working for me, because if my desire was to run a large organization, I had to show that I was capable. As general manager, I had approximately 450 people working for me, but I realized I needed to get up to the thousands level. Now, as president of all the operations in the United States, I oversee more than 8,000 people, and that is the level I had hoped to achieve at that time.

Even with this significant accomplishment, I still continue to revisit my career blueprint. This past year, I set my sights on becoming part of a corporate board. I immediately enrolled in a program at the Kellogg School of Management at Northwestern University specifically for minorities and contacted the Minority Director Development Program. Then I communicated with all the headhunters who find directors for companies to let them know I was interested. So while from a career perspective I have aspirations *within* my current organization, I have modified my blueprint to include working with *external* organizations in a board capacity.

KNOW YOUR STRENGTHS AND WEAKNESSES

When you are considering moving onward, it is important to be clear-eyed about what you do well, and what you *do not* do well. For example, in my first sales position, I took a sales training class at AT&T. After about six months, it was clear that some of my classmates were not skilled at selling. Because I was successful, many of my classmates asked me, "Hey, what do you do that makes you so successful?" I explained that one of my strengths was public speaking, yet many of my colleagues confessed they were uncomfortable making presentations.

When you are in sales, you *have* to give a lot of presentations. So if you are uncomfortable speaking in public in front of people, you are probably not going to be very good in sales. However, many of my fellow sales representatives who were not good in sales were very good with the details of putting together a deal. They excelled at creating solutions and configuring systems. Unfortunately, I was terrible at that; that was not what I did well. My attitude was if someone else could fix the widget, I could sell it.

So when my classmates came to me for advice on what they were doing wrong, I suggested, "Maybe you ought to consider sales support or solution development. You'll still get to meet with customers, but you won't be the lead dog. You won't be the person who has to make the deal happen. You'll be the person who *helps* the person make it happen." As a result, many of my classmates did move from sales to sales support or solution development, and they were much happier. Additionally, they were much more successful; being a salesperson is a high-pressure job, so the pressure was off them once they moved out of sales and they did not have to do a lot of the fronting, the public speaking.

Here is another example from my career: I am not a very detail-oriented person, but when you have P&L responsibility for $800 million worth of business, you need to know the details of the balance sheet. So I took a refresher course on cost accounting, financial accounting, and mergers and acquisitions to bone up on those areas that I dreaded. I did this two years ago—long after I had gotten my MBA, and when I was very far along in my career—because I realized that although I do not enjoy knowing the nitty-gritty of the financials, I had to for the position I wanted and now have.

KNOW YOUR PERSONALITY TRAITS

You also need to know which of your personality traits can help you at work, and which might get in the way of your climbing the corporate ladder. For example, Juan was a sales director at a Fortune 500 telecommunications company, but he was frustrated in his job. After we talked about the source of his frustration, what became very clear was that he did not like working with people. He does not like managing people; he is a lone ranger. But Juan had been such a good salesperson that someone talked him into becoming a sales manager and then the sales director. Essentially, he had moved on from doing something he had enjoyed and been successful at to doing something he *did not* enjoy and therefore *was not* successful at.

A suggestion was for him to consider moving to a company that has global account executives, who are each responsible for one very large account. They are responsible for running their own, and they get paid extremely well. Juan did not know such a position existed, because it did not at the company he was working for. But he realized that this was exactly the type of job that appealed to him, and that he would be successful at. So he joined a company that employed global account executives, and he is now the chief client officer for Bank of America. He is a one-man team. He has people who work with him, but they do not report to him; they work as sales support people. And the best thing is, he makes more money doing this than he ever did managing a team of people, and he is much happier. He recently called me and said, "Keith, that's the best thing you could have told me to do."

On the other hand, there are people who are very good at just talking—and that is a personality trait that can become a terrific career strength. For example, traveling on business, I stopped to work out at a fitness center in Alabama and met one of the personal trainers, Tanya. She was very personable and had great communication skills. Moreover, she was very knowledgeable about fitness: she really knew her product well. She also took the time, even though I was just a day visitor to this gym, to ask me what my fitness goals were and what I was most interested in working on. She helped me create a great workout routine to match my fitness goals. She was very impressive in her approach to her job, and would be a great salesperson in any field. I gave her my card and said, "I'm from Pitney Bowes. If you ever want to get into sales, give me a call." Tanya called me about two days later. I had already left town, but I forwarded her information to the sales director for the Alabama office, who hired her—and she won the sales representative of the year. Tanya had never sold a day in her life before, but her personality was such that she was great with people. She was a natural salesperson, but she did not even realize it until it was pointed out to her.

Still, even though she was smart, talented, and skilled, she got lucky, because she was offered a chance to capitalize on her strengths. Most people are not going to be that lucky, so you need to develop your own luck. Do not wait for someone to discover which of *your* personality traits can help you in your career: try to discover them for yourself.

KNOW WHAT YOUR PASSIONS ARE

You should also recognize what your true passions are. It really is true that if you do what you love, success will follow. For example, Lawrence was another manager who was working in operations, but was always going to diversity fairs and representing his company at diversity events. In fact, Lawrence spent so much time on his interest in diversity that he was failing in his day job. Honestly, he was actually on the verge of getting fired. He was written up and given a letter about his poor performance and was seeking counsel. We discussed if he had ever thought of going to HR and saying, "I'd like to be the diversity champion or the manager for diversity for our company, because that is my passion." He had not done this because he did not think HR would consider it, but he would never know until he asked. Lawrence did exactly that, and because he was a fifty-seven-year-old African American man, his company was willing to let him do that for the last couple years of his career. He became the company's "diversity director"; they actually created the position for him.

If you know what your passions are and can use them in your career, you too will be happier in what you are doing and better at what you do. Do not wait until someone else points this out to you. Instead, try to discover this on your own so you do not waste valuable years on a career path that is really a dead end for you in terms of what you *really* want to do.

LET NOTHING DISTRACT YOU FROM YOUR GOALS

Like many minorities, Richard Parsons, former chairman and CEO of Time Warner, did not get to the top without having to overcome his share of obstacles. Often I hear minority executives complain about the racism they feel they face on a daily basis. Because of self-doubt, some minorities actually psych themselves out of opportunities, believing either that they can't do a certain task or that others will doubt their ability and not offer them the chance.

Not being one who listens to doubters and naysayers, Parsons offered this advice in an interview with *Black Enterprise* magazine: "Eighty percent of what makes people successful is believing in yourself. A lot of people don't try because they are afraid to fail. Most people would rather follow than lead because it's safer." As for racism, real or perceived, "it's never particularly bitten me . . . but I know it's out there," he offered. "Blacks in the workplace are cut less slack, there's less tolerance for failure, particularly up front. It's a re-ality . . . it's just one of those things you manage.

"I do think there is something to the notion of a self-fulfilling prophecy . . . maybe some [motives] are [racist]," he added, "but to assume that all of them are, creates a sense of your own reality that will take you down a bad path."

ASSESS YOUR SKILL SET
(IT MAY NOT BE WHAT YOU NEED IT TO BE)

As mentioned earlier, you need to know what is required for the job you want. Then you need to honestly assess your skill set to deter-mine whether you have what that job requires. Let's look at Mau-reen's story. Maureen is the vice president of external affairs for Georgia-Pacific. Her position involves handling the company's char-itable contributions, some public relations, and other external com-munications for the company. Maureen wants to move into one of the business units and become vice president of a division. We dis-cussed the fact that she has a staff job, not a line job. And because she had no P&L experience, until she did and could show she can manage a budget successfully, no one was going to give her a shot at a C-level position.

We concluded that she would probably have to lose her vice presi-dent title and instead take a position with only the director title of a business unit—but with P&L responsibility. That way, she could earn her stripes and move up along that career path. Fortunately, in her case, she did not need to take finance courses, because she had an MBA. But it is one thing to have an MBA, and another to actually manage the drivers of revenue and expense for this year. She did not have that experience—and she needed to get it before she could move up to the type of job she wanted at the level she wanted.

KNOW WHERE YOU WANT TO GO WITH YOUR CAREER

You also need to know where you want to be when you retire, which goes back to creating your career blueprint. Most people graduate from college and have no idea what they want to do, and they just fall into something almost randomly. So when asked, "What do you want to be doing when you retire?" most people jolt at this question, because they have not thought that far ahead.

For example, Leslie has been a project manager for a high-tech company for several years. She came for advice and said, "Project management is great, but I do not want to do this for the rest of my life. I really want to do something more in the field of HR." It was pointed out that she was never going to get to HR by managing projects. So a plan was put together that would leverage her project management skills with HR.

Leslie proposed to HR that she run a project to address a particular problem her company was having with employee retention. She wanted to conduct a study and analysis of the problem and then propose some solutions based on the analysis. Her HR department agreed to let her do this to help the company understand why it is having this retention problem. She is still doing her project management job, but she has volunteered to take on the additional responsibility of this HR project on her own time. She is using her project management skills to analyze an HR problem, which is a terrific way for her to blend her experience and skills with what she ultimately wants to do. She is getting her foot in the door with HR.

Leslie has also considered how she might be able to actually parlay her project management experience into a job in HR at some future time. As discussed in chapter 3, to get to where you want to be in your career, you may need to take on special projects that will broaden your experience and your exposure to other departments in the company, other levels of the company, and other people in the company.

IDENTIFY WHAT OR WHO MIGHT HELP YOU GET WHERE YOU WANT TO BE

As mentioned previously, it is really important to become involved in professional organizations outside your company. Two that are worth recommending over and over again are the National Society of Hispanic MBAs and the National Black MBA Association. Moreover, if you acquire a leadership role in the local chapters of these organizations, that is even better for your career.

✦ How Volunteering Turned into a Job

When I had the privilege of serving as president of the Cleveland chapter of the National Black MBA Association (NBMBAA), I met Diane, who had an MBA but had been laid off and was looking for a job. Diane decided to volunteer for the NBMBAA as the director of business development. Note that this was an unpaid position, working in external relations. In this capacity, she did fund-raising and went to corporations to represent our organization. The reason she was asked to volunteer, even though she did not realize it at the time, was because it would give her the chance to meet with a lot of people at many more organizations and companies than she would have been able to meet on her own. The companies she met with saw how professional she was, and she was offered a job. Even volunteering can help you advance in your professional career.

Another benefit is that many organizations made up of volunteers allow you to make mistakes in a controlled environment. In other words, there is not as much at stake as when you are working in a corporate environment, where your job may be on the line with every deal you make or every project you take on. There are even executive development institutes where you can role-play to practice certain skills in a safe environment, as opposed to in a real job. For example, you do not want to give your first presentation ever in front of senior leadership at a new company. These organizations can give you the opportunity to try out these skills before you have to use them in your day-to-day job.

And in some cases, your volunteer work may even give you the opportunity to run a business and get some P&L responsibility and experience. For example, I encouraged the VP of global security at Pitney Bowes to take on the presidency of the Connecticut chapter of the NBMBAA for two important reasons: first, to increase his visibility, and second, because he does not currently run a large organization within Pitney Bowes. However, the Connecticut NBMBAA chapter comprises over a hundred people, so this volunteer position gives him the ability to document and talk about his ability to manage over a hundred people. This position has also sharpened his skill set not only because he is now managing and directing people, but also because he has P&L responsibility: the Connecticut chapter has a budget of about $100,000 for fund-raising and to run various community-based programs, including tutoring for underachieving teenagers.

The black and Hispanic MBA associations are just two examples of worthwhile organizations to become involved with. You should also look into organizations that are specific to your industry; for example, there is an organization of black data-processing professionals, there is an association of blacks in journalism—you name the discipline, it probably has its own unique organization that you can join to find a mentor and learn from others who are more seasoned in your business.

I have also suggested to many people that they should join the local Toastmasters organization to work on their presentation skills. They come back with comments such as, "Hey, I did that for a couple of years, and I became really comfortable speaking in public. Now I give great presentations." That's a terrific skill to have in any business and any company.

KEEP IN MIND YOUR LONG-RANGE CAREER GOALS

Earlier in this chapter, I advised you not to move to a different company just because the title or the pay is better in the short term, because that company may not be able to offer you the best *long-term* prospects. In the examples cited in those sections, those managers made bad decisions because they did not keep in mind their long-range goals. Fortunately, I have been able to offer advice to a few people *before* they made the wrong decision for their career.

✦ How Three Managers Handled Career Moves

Kenneth was a sales director in the computer industry in Chicago, when he was downsized from his company in 1999–2000. After working with a search firm, he was offered a VP-level job with Kodak. The job was in Rochester, New York, and it paid more than he had been making in his last job. However, he had some questions about whether he should take the job. On the one hand, Kenneth thought it was a great job, working for a great company. His biggest issue was that he did not want to relocate to Rochester.

Kenneth was right not to want to relocate, not because he did not like the city of Rochester, but because Chicago is obviously a much larger metropolitan area, and many more companies have regional offices or headquarters there, so his *future* opportunities for employment would be better if he stayed in Chicago. Even more important for Kenneth to consider was the trouble that Kodak was having in the marketplace at that time; film was becoming more and more obsolete, and Kodak was struggling to compete with digital camera technology. Kenneth thought long and hard, because he did not have another offer. But he did not want to relocate and he did not want to risk his future, so he turned down the Kodak job. He found a job eventually, and six months later, he learned that the division of Kodak in which he had been offered a position was ultimately eliminated in the next round of downsizing at Kodak.

Essentially, Kenneth kept in perspective what his current prospects would be even if he did not take the Kodak job. He was in a tough situation, because he had just been downsized from one company, and he was still dealing with the shock. And he was upbeat about the job Kodak was offering him and about Kodak in general. What brought him down to earth was considering the big picture, over the long term. He had to realize that although this might be a great job right now, if something happened to that great job and he was unemployed in Rochester, there were not many other employers there. If he stayed in Chicago, on the other hand, his long-term prospects were better. Also, he needed to look harder at the company and industry he was going to work for, because it was clearly declining.

. . .

Peter is a minority executive at a high-tech firm, in his late forties. A late starter in his career, he worked his way up and was offered a promotion to district director in New Orleans. Peter was hesitant to relocate because he was in Atlanta, which is one of the largest cities for his company in the area of sales, whereas New Orleans is a very small district for the company. He was encouraged to take the job for two reasons: first, because he was getting a promotion to director; and second, because New Orleans *was* a smaller district, and in this case, it would be easier for him to make an impact there. (Moving to a smaller district within the *same* company can often be a great career move, as this example shows. However, be wary of moving to a smaller company, as discussed earlier in the example of Nathan, who moved to a small company only to have his career completely stall because there was just nowhere to move up to: that manager should have stayed at his much larger company, where there were more opportunities to advance.)

Reluctantly, Peter accepted the position in June 2005. Then Hurricane Katrina hit in September 2005, and during the whole time after the storm, he provided exceptional leadership for the company as well as for his customers and his employees, and that leadership made a great impression on the CEO of his company. Because of his outstanding work in this "small" office, Peter was promoted only six months later to director of a larger district, back in Atlanta—so he got to go back to where he wanted to be in the first place. Taking the position in a seemingly small office actually proved to be the best decision he could have made.

Again, you need to keep in mind what your *long-term* goals are, and if you think that the next short-term position will get you closer to that long-term goal—even if the short-term job may not be exactly what you want to do right now—then you should take that job. This is also what Carl did when he took the lateral job offer and moved to Florida to head up his company's efforts in Latin America. He was out on the West Coast, but he agreed to move because he came to realize that the international experience was necessary for him to reach his long-term goal of climbing higher in the company. So he lived in Florida for two years, then was given the job he wanted.

• • •

The same was true for Leonard, a minority sales manager who was offered a lateral move from his company's regular phone system division to its new cellular division, which was opening up in the same city. At first, Leonard did not see the value of making this move; as he said, "It's a start-up, and I'll have to hire staff and rent space and develop retail presence." In other words, he really did not want to take on all that work. However, he needed to see how much stronger his résumé would read with all those new responsibilities. So he accepted the position, and two years later, Leonard was hired by a larger competitor to serve as general manager for one of that company's larger markets, and later he was made VP of an entire region.

Finally, keep in mind Kyle, the Cingular salesman I introduced to you in chapter 4, who ignored his long-term goals, accepted the short-term position that he wanted so badly, and almost lost his job because of this shortsightedness. Do not make the same mistake he did. Try to make career decisions that will help you to reach your ultimate goals over the long term.

CONSIDER WHETHER IT MAKES SENSE
FOR YOU TO CHANGE INDUSTRIES

In addition to all the other issues I have discussed so far in this chapter, I am often questioned by younger managers as to whether they should change industries to get ahead. This is a concern for young managers of any race. The answer to that question depends on the condition of the industry you are leaving versus the one you are considering moving to. Take the example of Kenneth, who considered leaving Chicago to take a great job at Kodak: even though the job seemed terrific, the company and the entire industry were struggling, so that move would have been the wrong decision.

Naturally, there are cases where moving to a different industry is the right decision to make. For example, John was VP of the pay-phone division of a large company in 1997. He contemplated a career change to executive recruiting. John was about thirty-five years old, and he was a director in that company, but he saw that the pay-phone industry was really declining as cell-phone technology was becoming more prevalent. He believed that because of his years of making contacts in the industry and his fondness for networking, recruiting would be a natural fit for him. So he left the pay-phone company and joined a minority executive search firm in Chicago, and he is doing quite well: in fact, John is now one of the firm's partners.

5

Career Killers You Must Avoid

Because Minorities Don't Get Second Chances

When Franklin Raines sat before Congress in the fall of 2004, his defense was very different from those who were summoned earlier to Washington to explain the unscrupulous accounting practices that caused the fall of Enron and WorldCom. The chief executives of those companies argued that they had no idea about the financial maneuvering that led their companies to ruin. Raines, however, an African American and the CEO of Fannie Mae, said that not only was he aware, but he approved the accounting practices at his company. In the end the Securities and Exchange Commission found Fannie Mae guilty of violating accounting rules, and the mortgage company's board replaced Raines. "Franklin Raines is a very decent human being," said Jeffrey A. Sonnenfeld, an associate dean at the Yale School of Management in an interview with *The New York Times*, "but he's lost the legitimacy to lead."

Unfortunately, these types of stories are covered regularly in today's business periodicals: key executives resigning or being forced to resign from their companies over a fatal mistake, a lapse of judgment, or, worse yet, illegal activity. In many instances the offender is a well-liked, highly respected, high-performing leader within the organization. But none of that matters when an executive's integrity is questioned. In fact corporations today, particularly because of the reckless management practices that caused the demise of Enron and WorldCom, and the extreme competitiveness in the marketplace, are much less accepting of any behavior that exposes the company to risk, diminishes its brand, or opens it up for scrutiny by federal regulatory agencies.

Why is this an issue for minorities? Because there are *no* second chances! Every senior leader throughout his career has designed a program, introduced a project, or planned a strategy that entailed varying levels of risk taking. In fact, it is almost impossible to reach senior levels of an organization without having demonstrated a strategy around risks. The possibility of failure or miscalculation is inherent in designing an evolutionary program for your company, opening an office in a region that your firm had resisted, or proposing to develop a new product or service outside the traditional core competencies of the company. But there is a clear difference between taking a strategic risk and taking chances.

THE "NO BRAINER" CAREER KILLER: UNETHICAL BEHAVIOR

It may prove challenging, depending on the size or the cost of a miscalculation, but most professionals can recover from a mistake in strategy. But there is little recourse for mistakes caused by bad judgment resulting in financial misconduct or even social and sexual misbehavior. It may seem quite elementary—even insulting—to warn professionals against illicit behavior, but many of the biggest cases in the news have involved criminal acts. Most professionals will not engage in schemes to deliberately defraud shareholders, but too many employees engage in unprofessional behavior that could damage their careers.

What many don't realize is that these acts don't usually occur in isolation; they are often tacitly encouraged or supported by the culture of an organization. If "everybody" uses the company credit cards for personal use "every once in a while," is that acceptable behavior? I know minority managers who were fired in such instances. Quite often, when these same mistakes were made by white managers, they were treated as serious abuses, but the white managers were not fired.

If members of your organization regularly engage in sexually offensive humor, it will probably continue, particularly if such behavior is never challenged. As a result, the behavior seems acceptable. That does not, however, make it excusable. If everyone decides to modify the dress code from professional to business casual, does that make it acceptable to the powers that be? I think not.

We have devoted an entire chapter in this book to the importance of becoming a team player to improve your status within an organization, but it is also important for minority employees always to maintain strong ethics and integrity in all manner of business. If accusations of illicit behavior are ever made against a company, your behavior should never be called into question.

Consider this real-life example: Two men in the same company were accused of three cases each of sexual harassment: the white manager's were confirmed, but the minority manager's weren't. Nevertheless, the white manager was offered retirement with full benefits. The minority manager was fired. Because I was intimately involved with the facts of all three cases, I can tell you there was enough evidence in each of the cases to indicate guilt—but in the end only the minority manager was fired.

Because more and more business is being conducted in social settings, out-of-office decorum must also be properly managed. In an environment where drinks are being served, music is playing, and colleagues are gathered, associates have to be both guarded and strategic in their behavior. Social encounters provide a dynamic opportunity to network, show a more socially engaging side of your personality, and allow you to gather information that might not be disclosed in a more formal setting. Reckless behavior in such a setting, however, can have long-lasting damaging effects on your career.

After several drinks, one minority manager began talking loudly at a company party and was described by another coworker as being obnoxious. She was called into HR. Her behavior was documented, and she was warned that if it happened again, she would be fired. Another minority manager was seen dancing somewhat suggestively at the company's holiday party; six months later, he was passed up for promotion because he lacked "business maturity." The decision was based on how he behaved at that party!

The bottom line is, if you're a minority, integrity is extremely important, and must be upheld at all times. Though you may have a legal right to claim discrimination if you are treated differently for committing the same violation as a nonminority, it is best not to commit the violation in the first place.

COACHING TIPS TO AVOID THE APPEARANCE OF "CODE OF CONDUCT" VIOLATIONS

- Avoid all situations that are inappropriate. For example, visiting an after-hours strip club with your sales team is a bad idea—even if the sales manager is leading the group.
- Arrange for potentially contentious meetings (particularly with those of the opposite sex) to be held in the office—not at dinner, not in a hotel suite (even when traveling with colleagues), not after working hours. If you are traveling, meet in a public location.
- Use your company credit card *very* judiciously. You might rationalize, "Everyone else takes a buddy to dinner from time to time and expenses it, why can't I?" Because you might get fired for it. It's really not worth losing your job over a $200 dinner with a friend from college.

THE REAL CAREER KILLER FOR MINORITIES: CAREER DERAILMENT!

Sexual misbehavior, as well as financial and social misconduct, are obvious career killers, but there are more subtle, less obvious indiscretions that claim many more corporate victims—and are unknowingly committed on a regular basis. The real career killers are less obvious, harder to put your finger on, and yet have the ability to totally derail a minority executive's career. For many minority professionals, the concept of career derailment is now only beginning to be clearly understood. In her book *Get Your Groove Back*, Jasbinder Singh, noted business psychologist and executive coach, says, "Career derailment is a common theme in the modern workplace today. I have coached clients who were seemingly 'hot property' one day only to find themselves on the scrapheap the next."

But what is career derailment? In his article "Derailment: What It Is, and What to Do About It!," executive coach David Montross writes, "Derailment is the organizational assessment of a manager that says, in effect, this manager has failed to live up to expectations. It is not the same as plateauing, nor is it when you decide to stop the upward climb and opt out of further advancement. Derailment is reserved for those who want to go onward and upward, but for whom the organization says 'enough.' " However, it is important to understand that derailment doesn't just happen. According to Don W. Prince, manager, Emerging Markets for the Center for Creative Leadership Europe, "derailment doesn't come out of the blue, striking at whim. In most cases, it can be predicted, and is usually the responsibility of both the individual manager and the organization." The Center for Creative Leadership (CCL), one of the world's largest organizations dedicated to the understanding, practice, and development of leaders worldwide, has pioneered research in this area and found that professionals who derail fall into several categories:

- Have difficulty changing or adapting
- Have problems with interpersonal relationships
- Fail to build and lead a team
- Fail to meet business objectives
- Have too narrow a functional orientation

Likewise, CCL research indicated that those professionals who are successful:

- Have greater diversity in their career paths
- Maintain good composure under stress
- Handle mistakes with poise
- Are focused problem solvers
- Get along with all kinds of people

So how can minority executives prevent derailment in their careers? Prince offers this advice: "The first step is to understand that leadership development is dynamic and on-going. The ability to learn and develop continually is a key competency in today's organizations. The manager needs to recognize that new jobs require new frameworks and new behaviors." These topics will be discussed in greater detail in chapter 6, "Must-Have Skills Every Senior Leader Needs."

DERAILMENT CHALLENGES
FOR THE YOUNG MINORITY PROFESSIONAL

At its Greensboro, North Carolina, campus, CCL offers specialized leadership development programs for mid- to senior-level women and minorities, and more information is available on their Web site, www.ccl.org. However, there are some "early warning" derailment factors that impact less seasoned professionals. Below are what I have identified as the primary derailment factors for entry- to mid-level professionals:

- Not understanding or documenting performance expectations.
- Not demanding and/or not accepting feedback, guidance, and direction.
- Not being able to quantify your value to your organization.

While some of these actions have more immediate consequences than others, over time they can all work to derail an otherwise promising career. Let's take a closer look at each.

1. Not understanding or documenting performance expectations. We have already explained the importance of performing at a high level in your existing role in order to excel in an organization. To be able to exceed performance expectations, you need to have a clear understanding of what they are. The first question I ask professionals who are frustrated with their stagnation within a company is, "When you started your position, did you get a clear, documented understanding of what your performance expectations were?" Most will then start to outline their job description. What many don't realize is that there is a distinct difference between the expected tasks you are required to perform in a given role (job description) and *how well* you are expected to perform those tasks over a defined period of time (performance expectation).

Performance expectations may also be referenced by several different names: MBOs (management by objectives), strategic architecture, compensation target objectives, or simply job goals. However they are defined, these are the metrics by which you will ultimately be *measured* to determine your effectiveness in a given role.

If these expectations are not documented and understood up front, employees leave themselves vulnerable to subjective observations of their management.

✦ Vinay's Dilemma:
Balancing Expectations

A few years ago, at a conference hosted by the National Society of Hispanic MBAs (NSHMBA), I had the opportunity to meet a young man named Vinay. Vinay was in the job market after only two years at a very well known consulting firm. He was frustrated because although he felt he had performed well in his last position, he felt discriminated against because of his "accent." He explained that he was very knowledgeable in his area of expertise, and that clients would often request that he be assigned to their projects. When I probed further, I discovered his blind spot: Vinay defined success as helping solve his clients' business problems and maintaining high customer satisfaction ratings.

He had not, however, understood that he was also expected to perform this work at a particular level for his employer, which included wrapping up projects quickly, reducing unbillable resources, and curtailing benefits offered to clients outside of the original scope of work. In the end, he created satisfied clients but delivered very little profit to his employer's bottom line. From the point of view of performance expectation, his focus was not clear on what defined success in his role.

✦ Sidney's Problem:
What's My Real Target?

After years of top performance, Sidney finally received her promotion to general manager of a copy center located in her company's largest market. Previously, she had worked as an assistant general manager in a smaller Midwest market. Thrilled to be in charge of the highest-revenue-generating store in the largest market, Sidney set out to prove she was the right choice for the job, and made it her goal to break the previous sales performance of her predecessor. Her boss's only advice was to make sure she outperformed her peers and, at the end of the year, captured the General Manager of the Year award at the company's annual recognition event.

To please her boss, Sidney worked tirelessly to grow sales revenue and exceed the previous year's sales numbers. Each month when Sidney and her manager reviewed the previous month's results, Sidney would focus almost exclusively on her sales growth. At the end of each session, her manager would remind her, "Make sure you outperform your peers and beat last year's numbers." However, at the end of the year Sidney was shocked to see a "Needs Improvement" rating on her annual review. Upset, she challenged her boss on the rating, showing him evidence that she had indeed exceeded the previous year's sales numbers. Her boss then informed her, "Yes, but you were over budget significantly in supplies, your customer satisfaction scores have dropped significantly, and your profit margin is 30 percent below the company average. You didn't do a complete job."

It was then that Sidney realized that she and her boss had completely different definitions of what success looked like in her new role, and she had never bothered to get it in writing. A quick study, Sidney made sure that she would not make the same mistake again!

COACHING TIP

Have your performance expectations put in writing. Work with your manager to clearly delineate and document what is expected of you in the way of measurable goals and targets for the year. Have him outline, if possible, what is acceptable performance as well as what is "exceptional" performance. Personally, I make sure my boss documents my performance expectations on a scale of 1 to 5 for my benefit. For example:

"1" Performance = Achieving greater than 120 percent of the target

"3" Performance = Achieving 100 percent of the target

"5" Performance = Achieving less than 90 percent of the target

By making sure we are both on the same page relative to my performance expectations, there is little chance for misunderstanding later in the year when it comes time for evaluations and pay raises.

2. Not demanding and/or not accepting feedback, guidance, and direction. The second biggest mistake I see minority executives make is not demanding feedback, guidance, and direction from their managers and mentors, and many times not accepting it when it is given.

Professional evaluations are offered two ways: formally and informally. Formally, they come from your direct manager or supervisor. Sometimes such feedback comes from a mentor who has been assigned to you in a structured mentorship program. You may also receive feedback from mentor relationships that have developed informally. Sponsors and other colleagues are among the best sources of feedback. It's important to note, however, that unless you seek feedback on your overall performance in a company, you may never get an honest assessment of your status in that company. Without knowing how you're perceived, it is almost impossible to exceed performance expectations and move your career to new heights. It's particularly important for minority professionals to seek such guidance. As we have noted in other chapters, studies show that many white supervisors and coworkers hold back on offering constructive criticism to minority subordinates for fear of being perceived as racist.

Unfortunately, many minority professionals also have biases attached to the idea of feedback. Early in my career, I mistakenly believed that to ask for guidance was a sign of weakness. In my mind, it implied that I was insecure and needed validation. To ask for direction was to suggest that I really lacked initiative and needed others to motivate me. To seek direction meant that I was lost, and didn't know where I was going. In addition, my generational bias had me believing that seeking help, particularly from a white male executive, would forever label me an "empty suit." It was ingrained in me *not* to reach out. As a result, I spent a great deal of time studying at the school of hard knocks! Lessons I could have learned in days took weeks. Skills I could have mastered in weeks took months. Commissions, awards, promotions, and bonuses I could have earned in months took years!

After many disappointing performance reviews, the turnaround for me came when a female manager of mine suggested that we review my performance on a quarterly schedule. While it was difficult at first, this one act of seeking feedback on a quarterly basis served to take me from being a "PoPo" (passed over and pissed off) to a "HiPo" (high potential) individual. As I moved up the corporate ladder, I continued to hold monthly one-on-one sessions with my manager to receive feedback, and with my direct reports to both give *and* receive feedback.

I eventually understood that any lesson I could learn, any mistake I could avoid, any skill I could develop, any performance I could improve, and any money, promotion, or bonus I could earn by taking the time to get input from others was more rewarding than the false pride that came with "doing it on my own." But I also learned that as well as seeking help and direction from superiors, I had to be receptive to the advice offered.

+ *Valerie's Story:*
A Quarterly Meeting Leads to a Promotion

My good friend Valerie was a sharp, successful sales manager at a major telecommunications company. She had a bachelor's degree from Spelman College and had worked her way up the ranks by being a sales wizard. During a review of her quarterly sales forecast, she caught the attention of a senior executive within her company. Impressed by her presentation skills, he requested a meeting to better understand her forecast. During this meeting he learned that Valerie had career goals to move out of sales into general management. Given that all her experience in the corporation was in sales, she had unintentionally become pigeonholed. She was seen as a great sales manager, not a general manager.

This senior executive offered her guidance on how to make the transition. First, he encouraged her to take advantage of the company's tuition reimbursement plan and earn her MBA. So that she could better understand company structure, he suggested that she set up half-hour individual meetings with the leaders of operations, finance, marketing, and strategy. This also helped her understand their particular challenges and provided insight into their requirements when seeking talent. Lastly, he suggested that she volunteer for any cross-departmental task force created to look at ways to improve the business.

Within four years of acting on this guidance and direction, Valerie not only made the leap from sales to strategic planning but enjoyed a two-level promotion to vice president in the process. To this day, she will tell you that none of this would have been possible without the guidance and direction of that senior executive. In fact, he made it his business to open doors for her once he noticed her commitment and saw that she welcomed his direction. Nobody smiled more when her promotions were announced than he.

COACHING TIPS

• At a minimum, have quarterly feedback sessions with your immediate manager to determine if there are any performance gaps, concerns, or help you may need to meet and exceed your performance expectations for the year. If possible, hold these sessions monthly as a one-on-one session.

• If this is not frowned upon in your company's culture, request an annual skip-level meeting with your manager's manager, as mentioned in chapter 3. As a point of definition, a skip-level meeting is one where you meet, typically for a half hour to an hour, with your boss's boss. The purpose of the meeting is not to "tell" on your boss, or to make personal requests or demands. Rather, it is more of a getting-to-know-you meeting where you can gain insight into what issues are facing senior management, and in turn share your ideas on how to improve business results. This type of meeting not only gives you added visibility but can also provide you with insight into what senior management looks for in a leader. This will prove invaluable when you are up for promotion in the organization.

• Make an effort to identify at least one senior leader either inside your company or outside of it to serve as your mentor. This individual should have a proven track record of excellence in the areas you feel are your "lesser strengths." Once a mentor/mentee relationship is in place, work on those areas of development until you feel you have moved to a level of competence.

• Even if you receive negative feedback or feedback you don't agree with, take the emotion out of it and objectively reevaluate the feedback.

3. Not being able to quantify your value to the company. As you move from middle to senior management, this career killer can be the most deadly. This is especially true if your company ever experiences a downsizing or restructuring. In the world of "value propositions," "value-added service," and "shareholder value," it is imperative that as a minority business executive, you be able to articulate a "personal value proposition" that is measurable and quantifiable.

Too often we evaluate our performance based on the tasks that we have accomplished. During my initial mentoring sessions I will typically ask my mentee the question, "What value do you bring your company in your current role?" In many cases, they struggle to find an answer at all. Other responses:

"I am one of the top sales executives in the company."

"I am the best recruiter in our HR department."

"My department has the highest customer satisfaction rating in the company."

"I have developed some of the most creative solutions for our customers."

"My marketing campaigns have been the most successful."

At first glance, these sound like very admirable accomplishments, but they are all missing one vitally important component. None of them is quantifiable, and as a result, they appear more subjective than fact-based. Additionally, none of them really identifies the value they provide to their organizations. If you can't prove your value, what are you worth to an organization? How expendable are you?

Business today is more bottom-line-focused than it has ever been. Companies are focused on providing shareholder value. CEOs and corporate boards spend much of their efforts making sure that the company's stock is attractive to Wall Street and the investment community. In years past, companies could court investors and satisfy shareholders with a great story regarding their three-to-five-year strategic plan. Today companies are being pressured to prove their value on a quarterly basis. It matters not that a company has had three successive quarters of growth. One bad quarterly report can send stock prices reeling!

Why is this important to you? Because just as corporations are being evaluated based on the quantifiable value they provide, they in turn make employment and career decisions based on the quantifiable value that each employee provides. And while the performance of some jobs is easier to measure in quantifiable terms than that of others, the better you can prove your worth, the better you can position yourself for promotions, key assignments, performance evaluations, or even a new job in the interview process. Furthermore, in these difficult times of right-sizing, downsizing, and outsourcing, effectively quantifying your value in a company can serve as "career insurance" when decisions are being made on who to keep and who to let go.

Regardless what your position is, there are results or expectations that define whether you are successful or unsuccessful in your role. Make it a priority to understand what those critical success factors are, and take the time to document them and measure your performance against them on a regular basis.

✦ *Diego's Story*

Diego was a charming Latino gentleman responsible for West Coast recruiting for a leading wireless company. Because of the high turnover the company was experiencing, Diego was hired from a competitor to stop the bleeding and improve the company's hiring and employee-retention efforts. Within a few months, Diego had implemented a new recruiting process that targeted teachers, local churches, and junior college students. He implemented a new part-time position focused on recruiting stay-at-home moms and dads, allowing them to work while their kids were in school. Lastly, he hired an outside consultant to create a revised "new hire" training program that highlighted all of the great benefits the new hires would receive after ninety days on the job.

The company's store managers and sales managers were singing his praises. They noticed that the new employees were happier, better trained, and less likely to leave than in the past. However, the company's chief financial officer (CFO) noticed something else. Since Diego arrived, training costs had increased 50 percent, part-time labor costs had increased 30 percent, and because he increased part-time pay by 15 percent to be more competitive, salaries had increased as well. Armed with this information, the CFO summoned Diego to his office. He chewed Diego out for mismanaging company funds and not having a handle on expenses. He went on to inform Diego that unless he got his act together, he would have to consider recommending he be demoted from manager of recruiting to just a regular recruiter. Diego had no answers for his CFO. In fact, everything the CFO said was correct. However, Diego hadn't taken the time to *quantify* the value of his decisions. Had he done so, he could have shared with his CFO that he had reduced employee turnover by 50 percent, that he had reduced the time to onboard a new hire from two weeks to five days, and that by replacing full-time workers with part-timers where it made sense, he had actually reduced medical expenses by 15 percent, since the company didn't have to pay for medical coverage for part-timers. Imagine how differently that conversation could have ended if Diego had taken the time to quantify his value to the company!

. . .

Let's revisit those earlier answers I received from my mentees to see how much impact they offer when restated in *quantifiable* terms.

Original response: "I am one of the top sales executives in the company."

Restated: "This past year I brought in over $1 million dollars of new business to my organization."

Original response: "I am the best recruiter in our HR department."

Restated: "I have saved the company over $300,000 in recruiting costs by filling open position requisitions in thirty days or less, as opposed to the company average of forty-five days."

Original response: "My department has the highest customer satisfaction rating in the company."

Restated: "My department improved client retention by 50 percent as the result of improving our customer satisfaction scores 20 percent over the previous year."

Original response: "I have developed some of the most creative solutions for our customers."

Restated: "As a solutions architect, I have developed several applications that have increased my clients' productivity by 30 percent, and increased my company's revenue by over $500,000 this year alone."

Original Response: "My marketing campaigns have been the most successful."

Restated: "My creative marketing programs have helped improve our client retention by over 25 percent, and have helped our sales department add over fifty new clients this year."

Now imagine that you are sitting next to a key senior executive from your company at the annual holiday party, and she asks, "So what do you do for us?" Which answer from the list above do you think would most catch her attention? Envision being up for a promotion; during the interview you are asked, "So why do you think you are ready for such a demanding new role?" Which answer do you think would resonate most after completing the interview? If your company were downsizing, and trying to determine who to keep and who to let go, which answer would increase your chances of being retained?

While in sales at IBM, I learned to make myself invaluable to my clients by employing several tactics:

- Making sure I knew their business as well as they did.
- Knowing what their major issues and challenges were.
- Solidifying relationships with key decision-makers.
- Ensuring that these decision-makers were aware of the quantifiable value my solutions and service meant to their business:
  –My new solution reduces energy costs by 25 percent.
  –The new software helps your agents handle five additional clients an hour.

–Your new personal computers cost 15 percent less and have twice as much memory.

–The new printers use 30 percent less toner than your older units.

I would argue that these initiatives are equally useful *within* your organization, affecting your career growth and advancement.

COACHING TIPS

- Always identify the critical success factors (CSFs) for the role you are in. These are the results, expectations, and outcomes that, if achieved, would document you as being a success in that role.
- As best you can, measure and quantify your performance against these CSFs; discuss your performance against these CSFs on a regular basis (quarterly at a minimum) with your immediate manager, and annually with your boss's boss, if possible.
- When describing yourself and the role you play, never identify yourself with just a job title. Instead, always talk in terms of the value you provide.
- When creating an external or internal résumé, always begin with a section entitled "Key Accomplishments" that over four or five key bulleted points highlights your key successes in quantifiable terms.

6

Must-Have Skills
Every Senior Leader Needs

And Why They Are Even More
Important for Minorities

In today's highly competitive workplace, companies are constantly focused on identifying, recruiting, developing, and retaining the most highly skilled individuals they can. Given the need to compete not only on a domestic level but also globally, most Fortune 500 companies are in a race to develop leaders with the skills, talent, and ability to drive growth, improve financial performance and profitability, enhance innovation, and ultimately increase shareholder value. It is not uncommon for a company to hire retained executive search firms and pay them hundreds of thousands of dollars to find individuals who possess those ideal skills, and place them in senior leadership positions. Unfortunately, many minority managers have no idea what these crucial "hidden" skills required at the senior level are, and as a result they can spend their entire careers locked in mid-level positions. They may erroneously conclude that they are victims of the "glass ceiling," "concrete ceiling," or good-old-boys network, when in fact no one has ever taken the time to tell them what these executive-level skills are, and how to develop them.

WHAT ARE THESE SKILLS?

Every senior-level executive has his own personal hierarchy of traits and skills necessary to reach the C-suite, and I will offer several in this chapter. But of all the CEOs I have ever met or worked for, none has been as instrumental in providing me coaching and challenging me to grow as Murray Martin, chief executive officer of Pitney Bowes Corporation. The underlying thread for Martin is leadership, which in today's fast-paced global environment easily distinguishes the good executives from the great. "Over the years I have come to realize that leadership is an action and not a position," he explains. "Remarkable leaders help move the organization forward by virtue of their personal and professional attributes, not by virtue of where they sit on the organizational chart. These skills are truly leadership in action." Martin looks for several specific traits when identifying prospective company leaders:

1. **Strategic visioning:** Recognizing the future when you see it.
2. **Execution:** The ability to make things happen.
3. **Authentic leadership:** The ability to engage and energize others.
4. **Flexibility and adaptability:** Being able to manage multiple priorities.
5. **Awareness/political judgment:** The ability to navigate organizational boundaries.
6. **Personal accountability:** Taking ownership of decisions and actions.

"I have found that effective senior leaders demonstrate these skills irrespective of race, gender, age, culture, or life experience," says Martin. "The unfortunate reality, however, is that the less inclusive the environment, the more the minority leader has to prove on a regular basis that he/she has these capabilities. Be mindful that you will be tested frequently."

Because this is where many minorities lose traction in their career, it is important that we examine these skills from a variety of perspectives. To accomplish this, in addition to my own personal observations, I will provide insight from Kenneth Chenault, chairman and chief executive officer of American Express, as well as sharing input from a study sponsored by the Executive Leadership Council that combines the collective insight of fifty senior-level minority executives. By taking a collaborative view of how senior leaders define these must-have skills, it is possible to consider many different perspectives while determining how to customize and enhance your own skills development plan.

✦ Joseph's Story:
Sales Skills versus Management Skills

A few years ago, while working for a leading technology company, I was charged with identifying key sales professionals within the organization who had potential to move into general management. The company was focused on becoming more growth-focused. Instead of having business units led by engineering types who tended to focus more on "building a better mousetrap," the idea was to take individuals with a stronger sales background and place them in leadership roles, given their tendency to drive growth. Joseph was a minority sales manager who had enjoyed over fifteen years of sales success within the company. Beginning as a sales rep and moving into sales management, he had been recognized every year for his abilities to drive sales results. Because of this, he was immediately selected for a year-long leadership development program designed to give sales leaders the skills required to be successful business leaders. This program focused on financial reporting, driving productivity improvements, supply chain economics, and other skills that would be necessary to lead an organization.

During the program, Joseph struggled with many of the concepts pertaining to the financial aspect of running a business. However, he completed the program, and began interviewing for the general manager positions that had become available within the company.

During the interviews, Joseph focused almost exclusively on his track record of success in driving sales results. While this was impressive to the senior leaders he interviewed with, they were all very concerned with his inability to provide examples of how he would manage the business from a profit-and-loss (P&L) perspective, and his challenges in even understanding the importance of profitable growth. Since I was overseeing the program, I was asked my opinion of Joseph's ability to do the job. My honest assessment was that he could do the job, but would need additional coaching around the financial drivers. With my blessing, Joseph was made general manager of one of the company's larger Midwest markets.

Within a matter of months, it became obvious to all that not only was Joseph not focusing on the financials, he was not even interested in them. His main focus and passion was improving sales performance. The problem was, even though he was driving sales performance and growing revenue, because he was not focused on the financials, his profit margins had dropped from 40 percent to less than 15 percent. As a result, in only a year's time, Joseph was taken out of the general manager role. In the end, he and I both learned a valuable lesson. He learned that to be a *business* leader requires more than focusing on selling. I learned that I can never downplay the importance of critical business skills when mentoring or recommending a minority for senior leadership positions.

DIFFERENT SKILLS REQUIRED AT DIFFERENT LEVELS?

One of the biggest surprises many minorities face when they move up in corporate life is that the skills that made you successful in the past do not guarantee success in the future. This can actually be traced back to the college experience. While it takes a certain amount of dedication to earn an undergraduate degree, the basic skill is being able to listen to the professor's lecture, do your necessary reading and research, and ultimately test your ability in either a written or an oral exam. However, the classroom is an isolated environment. Once you graduate and begin working in the real world, you quickly learn that "textbook" knowledge will take you only so far. In fact, it can even be a hindrance to success if you are not flexible enough to apply your practical experience to what you have learned in class.

The same holds true once you are in a corporation. When you are an individual contributor, it is not as important to have developed your people skills. For example, you can be a successful salesperson or analyst all by yourself. However, to make the move into management you must very quickly cultivate people-management skills to begin to work through others to achieve a common goal. I am no longer amazed at the stories of successful salespeople who fail miserably at sales management, all because they have never developed the ability to lead and direct people.

Taken to its logical conclusion, the skills required for a good manager or director are not necessarily enough to make you successful at the vice president level. Just as the talent improves from the high school level to the college level to the professional level in the world of sports, the same holds true in the game of corporate life: the higher the position, the higher the skill level required to be successful. Coincidentally, just as the leap from college sports to professional sports is greater than the leap from high school to college, the skill level required to move from middle management to senior management is far greater than the move from entry level to mid-level management.

THE TOP FIVE SKILLS REQUIRED FOR SENIOR LEADERSHIP

Arguably, there are dozens of skills that can be identified as critically necessary for a senior leader. Over the years, however, I have discovered that five skills are identified more often than others by most who address this subject:

- Effective communication and presentation skills
- Analytical thinking and problem-solving skills
- Consensus-building/stakeholder management skills
- Solid financial acumen
- Ability to execute

It could be argued that this list contains seven or even eight skills, as the first three contain multiple references. However, looking more closely, you will discover that these particular skills typically go hand in hand, and combined they drive the same result.

EFFECTIVE COMMUNICATION
AND PRESENTATION SKILLS

Recently, after speaking to a group of minorities on the importance of excellent presentation skills, I was approached with the question, "What skill do you believe is the most important for minorities, and why?" Expecting some sort of long, intellectual response, they were stunned by the briefness of my answer: "Communication skills—because if you don't display these, you may never get the opportunity to display the others." The uncomfortable reality is, the perception is that minorites don't speak or write well. After years of television and movies displaying stereotypes of the ghetto-slang-talking African American, the broken-English-speaking Latino, or the difficult-to-understand Middle Easterner, many in the business world expect the same when these individuals walk into the room. In fact, for minorities, even your nonverbal communications can be misconstrued.

I still have the experience where I'll give a speech or a presentation, and many people come up to me afterward and compliment me on the way that I speak. Subconsciously or consciously, they don't believe that a black man will be well educated and well spoken. They don't intend to insult me with this stereotype; they truly intend to compliment me, but I know where that compliment is really coming from: it comes from a stereotype that minority managers will not be as articulate as our white counterparts. (This is similar to how Senator Joe Biden recently described Senator Barack Obama as the "first mainstream African-American who is articulate and bright and clean and a nice-looking guy." Unbelievable!)

Needless to say, if you want to make it past the cover letter to the interview, past the interview to the job, and past the job to a promotion and into the boardroom, you absolutely *must* take the time to cultivate and develop impeccable communication and presentation skills.

If you subscribe to the theory that first impressions are made within the first few minutes of contact, you would have to agree that excellent communication skills are imperative for today's senior leader. In today's multilevel communications world, with its Black-Berrys, e-mails, voice mails, and other communication devices, a leader is faced with more channels through which to share thoughts, ideas, and directives than ever before. To be effective, you need to make sure you communicate in a concise, clear, and articulate manner. For the purposes of this discussion, we will look at two forms of communication, oral and written. We will not address a third communication skill, nonverbal communication, here, but it can also be a very powerful component.

Oral Communication Skills

As a senior leader, you will be required to share your ideas, thoughts, and opinions during meetings, conference calls, or one-on-one with peers, subordinates, and bosses. During these times it is essential that you be able to speak in a manner that conveys confidence. Your thoughts must be articulate, logical, concise, and well thought out. Very often the success of a project or initiative can rest upon your ability to speak in a way that is convincing. To achieve this, it is important to focus on two elements: *what* you say, and *how* you say it. We have all been in meetings or on conference calls when someone attempts to share an idea or offer a comment, and after he has finished, you have no idea what he just said. Immediately, that person has made an impression in your mind that he is not very competent. Well, the reality is, the same holds true for you when you speak. People are listening to you to determine if you are competent, and whether you know what you are talking about.

Oral Communication Mistake 1: Taking too long to make your point. At the senior executive level, executives are busy, and time is their most valuable asset. This being so, it is important to be able to communicate your thoughts in a concise, direct, and logical manner. Too often, in an effort to impress, many managers will attempt to share everything they know on a subject during an interaction with a senior leader. More often than not, this will only give the senior leader the impression that you are not able to focus on the key facts and that you have no respect for his time. An example of this was a recent meeting I witnessed in which a manager was asked to provide an update to his executive vice president (EVP) on the latest customer satisfaction survey results. During the meeting, the manager went through excruciating detail that was of no real use to the EVP. After his presentation, the EVP thanked the manager for the update and excused him from the meeting. Later the EVP would remark that he had never heard such a confusing update in his life, and never again did he want that manager to present to him.

Oral Communication Mistake 2: Not being clear. Recently, I needed to review how well our business was doing with driving operational discipline into the culture. Several managers were assembled to share how their particular regions were doing in this area. One by one, they all spoke in acronyms that they didn't bother to explain, shared facts and figures that appeared to have no correlation, and in the end, never really answered my original request. I took this as a coaching opportunity and explained to each of them the importance of being able to logically and concisely communicate to me.

Later I also gave each of them a book by Milo O. Frank entitled *How to Get Your Point Across in 30 Seconds or Less*. In later meetings, I am pleased to report, they had all taken heed.

Written Communication Skills

More and more, with the increased use of technology in the workplace, today's manager will find it necessary to communicate effectively on many levels. While much focus is placed on oral communications, it is often in the area of written communications that many managers are challenged. From memos to proposals, cover letters, and e-mails, each and every day you will be called upon to display your ability to communicate effectively in writing. What some fail to realize is that with every word you write, you are making a statement about yourself, and an opinion of you is being formed. In an April 2005 *DiversityInc* magazine article entitled "If You Spel Like This, Your Career Is In Truble," C. Stone Brown warns that the inability to write well in business can have severe consequences: "written communication skills can keep an executive from being hired and promoted . . . and sometimes can lead to termination." It is vital that minorities take particular care to display excellent business communication skills given the perception issues that they face on a daily basis. The article later goes on to quote Nancy Flynn, executive director at ePolicy Institute, who says, "Every piece of written communication, whether it's a quick email or a formal letter, counts. People are forming judgments of you and your ability to communicate."

✦ *Angelo's Story:*
A Good Review Gone Bad

During a succession planning meeting, senior leaders held a special session to review a list of high-potential minority candidates. Though he did not realize it, Angelo was selected to be on the list based upon his last two years' performance as a financial analyst. As part of the succession planning process, he had to complete a standard form highlighting his accomplishments and strengths, and offering insight into what his ideal next job might be. Additionally, his immediate manager would offer commentary on how the candidate performed in his current role. Initially, there was a great deal of excitement about Angelo as the senior leaders read the glowing comments written by Angelo's manager. However, there was an uneasy silence in the room when the group read Angelo's commentary on himself. Not only were his comments long and rambling, they were filled with both grammatical and spelling errors. The group asked, How could a person who has accomplished so much not be able to articulate it in a logical manner that makes sense? Moreover, because Angelo hadn't even taken the time to use grammar-check or spell-check, the group concluded that he lacked attention to detail and determined he was not ready for a promotion in the near future. The ultimate tragedy is that Angelo had missed an opportunity to advance without ever realizing that he had the opportunity. What's worse, unless he gets feedback on his poor written communications skills, he will more than likely make the same mistake next year.

• • •

It is important in written as well as oral communication to make certain that your comments are logical, concise, and easy to understand. In the case of written communication, it is important that both the grammar and the spelling are correct, so you do not distract from your message and make the document more difficult to read. As a formal salesperson, and one who reads dozens of sales proposals today, I can tell you that a poorly written proposal will not only hurt your image and that of your employer, but may very well get you removed from the bidding process.

Brown's article closes by offering the following checklist for business writing:

A BUSINESS-WRITING CHECKLIST
- **Purpose.** Will the reader know—early—why you are writing?
- **Content.** Keep the intended reader in mind.
- **Organization and layout.** Does each idea transition logically from the previous idea?
- **Paragraph structure.** Does each paragraph make one major point?
- **Style and tone.** Is the language specific, natural, and appropriate to the reader?
- **Mechanics.** Is the grammar correct throughout? Are all the words spelled correctly?
- **E-mail.** Is your message as professional as a regular letter?

Remember, what you write speaks for you when you are not in the room to speak for yourself. You want to make sure that you do not destroy a brand you've taken years to create by crafting a poorly written, misspelled document.

Presentation Skills

If you ask almost anyone to create a list of their fears or the things they dread the most, speaking in public will almost always make the top three. It's as if from childhood we are tormented by the idea of standing in front of a group of people and speaking. It is easy to understand why this fear exists. No one wants to run the risk of being embarrassed or looking inept in front of a room full of strangers. Furthermore, unless you grew up speaking in public at school (thank you again, Ms. Caputo, for making me do this in grade school) or in your local church, few of us have had the opportunity to develop this skill. From a career perspective, it is possible to be successful and enjoy a prosperous career without ever developing this skill. However, if you desire to move into senior leadership positions, it is a skill that you, particularly as a minority, must develop.

The number-one reason you should develop and hone your presentation skills is that speaking in public allows you to demonstrate to senior leadership and others who you are and how well you understand the subject matter on which you are speaking. An additional benefit is that because most people *avoid* the opportunity to speak in front of a group, doing so says a great deal about your level of confidence, a trait many senior leaders look for.

✦ *How Good Presentation Skills Can Help Your Career*

Less than six months into my career at Pitney Bowes, in my role as area vice president I was asked to speak at an annual recognition event held in San Juan, Puerto Rico. The audience was made up of every senior leader in Pitney, various members of the board of directors, and more than three hundred top sales and service professionals and their spouses and significant others. As I was new to the company, not many people knew who I was, and as the only minority addressing the group, I was concerned about the impression that I would make on others. With less than six months on the job, I determined I would not come across as credible if I talked about industry-related matters, so instead I decided to draw from my experience at AT&T and IBM. Because I worked at both organizations during a time of major transition (AT&T during the divestiture of the Bell System, and IBM as it reinvented itself from a hardware manufacturer to a service provider), I was able to draw parallels between the journey those companies took and that of Pitney Bowes. After much rehearsal, I delivered a passionate speech that resonated with everyone in the audience. Afterward, I was approached by not only the CEO but also several board members in attendance, who congratulated me on such a fine job. The end result was that everyone knew who I was, and it opened the door for greater visibility within and outside the company. To this day, I am often asked by our CEO and our corporate communications group to speak on behalf of Pitney Bowes at both internal and external functions and with our board of directors.

What Makes for a Good Presentation?

The rules for a good presentation are similar to those mentioned earlier during the discussion on oral communications: it needs to be concise, logical, articulate, and well thought out. However, for a presentation I would add another trait: you must be *engaging*. While I will leave it up to the experts at Toastmasters and others to provide expert opinion on what it means to be engaging, as someone who has listened to my fair share of presentations, I can tell you that a speaker who is engaging is more likely to capture my attention than one who is not.

COACHING TIPS

- If you struggle at business writing, consider taking continuing education courses on written communication in business.
- Make sure you spell-check and grammar-check all e-mails and documents prior to sending.
- When preparing for a meeting, write down any key thoughts or ideas ahead of time so that you may deliver them clearly and concisely during the meeting.
- To enhance your public speaking abilities, consider joining your local chapter of Toastmasters International, or take classes on public speaking at your local college or university.
- Always rehearse your presentation several times alone or with a trusted partner before delivering it in public.
- Once you are comfortable speaking, take advantage of every opportunity you can to present to senior leadership.

ANALYTICAL THINKING AND PROBLEM-SOLVING SKILLS

As a business leader you will be expected to create strategies, drive change, and solve problems on a daily basis. As a regular employee or manager, you are generally expected to follow or implement the strategies handed down from senior management. As a senior leader, you will be expected to *create* those strategies. To do so, you must become skilled at looking at a problem, analyzing the facts, and determining a course of action to achieve the desired results. Too often in a corporation you will have many who are skilled at identifying a problem, but seldom can these same individuals come up with a solution for the problem.

As a minority, you need to set yourself apart from the pack by demonstrating skills in the area of analytical thinking and problem-solving. Given that companies are always faced with challenges, opportunities, and threats to the business, they are increasingly looking for leaders who have the ability to identify these business dynamics and create solutions that allow them to take advantage of opportunities, minimize threats, and meet business challenges head-on. Typically, they look for leaders who can:

- Translate opportunities, challenges, and threats and create business strategies and plans to achieve meaningful results.
- Balance the realities of short- and long-term business priorities and create action items that address both.
- Understand the need for change in the business, and anticipate the impact of change on the organization.
- Exercise sound judgment and logic in making decisions.

While the list could continue, the point is, to move from being a follower to a leader requires that you demonstrate an ability to identify and solve problems, and have a strategic focus on the entire business, not just your part of the organization.

COACHING TIPS

- Whenever possible, take part in a cross-departmental task force assigned to solve a company-wide business problem.
- Take time to understand the rationale for any merger or acquisitions your company may be involved in.

- Arrange for a meeting with a senior leader to understand the top three challenges she faces, and report back to her your thoughts on how to solve them.
- Take a course on business problem solving from your local college or university.

CONSENSUS BUILDING/STAKEHOLDER MANAGEMENT SKILLS

I recently came across an October 2004 *Harvard Business Review* article by Michael Porter that offered advice for new CEOs, entitled "Seven Surprises for New CEOs." In it, Porter identified seven surprises that new CEOs discover after taking their new roles. While they were all very relevant and helpful, one in particular stood out to me: "You can't run the company." The premise is that, given the demands placed on a new CEO by analysts, industry groups, board members, and the like, it is next to impossible to actually have hands-on, day-to-day involvement with the company operations. This being so, Porter states that it is important for the new CEO to understand three important lessons:

1. You must learn to manage organizational context rather than focus on daily operations.
2. You must recognize that your position does not confer the right to lead, nor does it guarantee the loyalty of the organization.
3. You are still only human.

While these lessons hold particularly true for new CEOs, they are worth noting for any senior leader. To be successful, you must learn how to accomplish your objectives by working *with* and *through* others. You need to be able to work *across* an organization, develop relationships and partnerships, and build consensus among peers—and sometimes even among enemies. Many middle managers have been successful with small teams, but senior managers need to be able to build collaboration on a much larger scale, and corporate politics become much more critical to success. It is important that you, as a minority, develop relationships at various levels within the corporation. Your network should not be limited to those in your business unit or discipline. As a senior leader you will be expected to:

- Develop networks and collaborate across the organization to drive business goals.
- Provide clear goals and objectives that others can understand and implement.
- Remove barriers to help teams function more effectively.
- Make connections with multiple constituencies to understand their needs and capabilities.
- Create a shared vision, and be able to have others embrace it.

It is impossible for you as a leader to make every decision, implement every strategy, handle every challenge, or solve every problem by yourself. The extent to which you are able to build networks, create teamwork, and inspire others to champion your cause will determine if you are in fact a leader that people follow because they *have* to, or because they *want* to. And in difficult times this difference will be reflected in the level of effort they give in support of the goal.

Why Interpersonal Skills Matter:
A View from the Executive Leadership Council

As mentioned in chapter 1, in June of 2006 members of the Executive Leadership Council (ELC) met in Savannah, Georgia, to revisit a study it had conducted in 1991 whereby fifty of its members were interviewed in an effort to create a "blueprint for success." These executives, who held positions of president, vice president, general managers, and directors within their companies, shared their thoughts and insights on everything from the "Indicators of Success" to the "Forces That Impact Success." The group not only identified communication skills as the number-one skill (see table on page 124) a minority must master to become successful, but also gave insights into how interpersonal communications skills help tremendously in building consensus:

• "While communications skills contribute to the success of all executives, the African American executives in this study felt that skillful multi-level communications were more critical to their success by bridging cultural gaps, overcoming racial obstacles, and gaining acceptance by their white counterparts."

• "African American executives . . . must rely on their interpersonal and collaborative skills to exert influence in order to avoid backlashes and labels such as 'pushy,' 'too aggressive,' 'difficult to work with,' and 'going too far.'"

While this study focused on African American executives, I believe this applies to other minority groups as well.

FACTORS CONTRIBUTING TO SUCCESS

Agreement	Percentage
Communication skills	100%
Leadership skills	
Self-presentation skills	
Team-building skills	
Ambition	98%
Hard work and long hours	
Interpersonal skills	
Management skills	
Problem-solving skills	
Innovation	
Luck or right place/right time	95%
Risk taking	
Knowledge of organizational environment	93%
Family support	91%
Time management	89%
Mentors	85%
Stress management skills	84%
Affirmative action/EEO	82%
Clear goals	80%
Career planning	76%
Company culture	54%
Company politics	53%

1991 Executive Leadership Council

These insights offer a unique glimpse into the challenges that these executives faced in their rise to the top, and that many still face today. Several executives emphasized that "comfort" and trust-building skills were more critical to minorities and women in overcoming barriers of being different. However, it was interesting and refreshing to hear these same executives stress that no minority should ever compromise her values or impair her identity in an effort to "fit in."

FORCES THAT IMPACT SUCCESS

Driving Forces	Restraining Forces
CORPORATE LIFE	CORPORATE LIFE
Interpersonal skills	Racism and sexism
Leadership skills	Discrimination/prejudice
Communication skills	"Concrete ceiling"
Ambition	"Old boys' network"
Hard work/long hours	Pay differential
Understanding environment	Restructuring/downsizing
Affirmative action / EEO	Company culture
Performance	Assertiveness/risks
Mentoring	Backlash
Manage diversity	Being limited to staff position
Self-confidence/esteem	
Assimilation/fitting in	
PERSONAL LIFE	PERSONAL LIFE
Core values/work ethics	Value conflicts
Education and experience	Generalists vs. specialists
Early family/social experiences	Job frustrations/derailment
Good health	Health issues
FAMILY LIFE	FAMILY LIFE
Time with family	Lack of family time
Supportive family	Concerns for family
Extended family influences	Frequent transfers
COMMUNITY LIFE	COMMUNITY LIFE
Involvement	Isolation
Recognition	Lack of time
	Demand for participation

1991 Executive Leadership Council

SOLID FINANCIAL ACUMEN

Being able to demonstrate that you understand the revenue and profitability drivers of a business goes a long way in positioning you for career success. Nothing helps you display this talent better than having solid financial acumen. This includes having the ability to understand the mechanics of an income statement and balance sheet, and being able to manage in such a way that you positively leverage these reporting tools to enhance company performance.

Unfortunately, unless you have at a minimum a degree in finance or accounting, the concept I mention above has no real meaning to you. However, if you have aspirations of ascending the corporate ladder, you will have to not only understand but *master* these concepts! If the acronyms EBIT or EBITDA mean nothing to you, you have a ways to go on this journey. Are you comfortable talking about gross margin, net margin, or ROI (return on investment)? If not, you will need to learn to be comfortable.

The reality is, while there are many positions that can be high-profile within an organization, such as director of diversity, VP of human resources, or VP of corporate communications, there is one thing that they all lack that is needed to reach the executive suite: line of business profit-and-loss (P&L) responsibility. These are the individuals who run a division or department of the corporation, and have revenue and profit targets that they must meet. They are, in fact, the "owners" of the business. Their success and that of the company depends on how well they manage their P&L responsibility. Because their results have such a direct impact on the financial health and, ultimately, the stock price of the corporation, they tend to have a great deal of clout within the company.

What If You Don't Manage a P&L?

The good news is, even if you don't have P&L responsibility, there is still a way to make yourself invaluable to your company: always be able to quantify your contribution! In most of my career, I have been fortunate enough to be in either sales positions or jobs in which I managed a P&L. In both cases, it was always apparent what my contribution was. In sales, I could quantify the value of either the new business I brought in, or the existing business I helped retain. Being over a P&L is, by definition, a job that quantifies your contribution. But what if your job is in recruiting, marketing, or training? Even in these roles there are still ways to quantify your contribution! In recruiting you can track key metrics like time to fill open positions, or your retention rate on new hires. In marketing, it could be the percentage take rate on your latest telemarketing campaign, or the amount of leads generated by the new collateral you created. In training, you could track the improvement in sales results after implementing the new sales training, or the reduction in benefits cost after rolling out the new benefits training. Whatever your role, there are always key outcomes that you can track and measure. As a minority, you want to be able to quantify your value to the business at all times.

ABILITY TO EXECUTE

Years ago, I heard it said that there are three types of people who work in companies today: those who *watch* things happen, those who *make* things happen, and those who have *no idea* what's happening. Corporations are full of people who are willing to watch things happen, and they even have a good number of workers who have no idea what's happening. However, they are also looking for those who are willing and able to *make* things happen. In their *New York Times* best-selling book *Execution: The Art of Getting Things Done*, authors Larry Bossidy and Ram Charan describe execution as "a systematic process of rigorously discussing the hows and whats, questioning, tenaciously following through, and ensuring accountability. It includes making assumptions about the business environment, assessing the organization's capabilities, linking strategy to operations and the people who are going to implement the strategy, synchronizing those people . . . and linking rewards to outcomes."

It's not enough to have crafted a compelling proposal, deliver an impressive PowerPoint presentation, or even design perfect project plans. When all is said and done, it boils down to execution. Have you demonstrated that you can take that proposal, presentation, and plan, and then, through execution, *deliver* the anticipated results? Until you have a track record of success in execution, your brand is not complete.

COACHING FROM THE C-SUITE

As mentioned earlier in this chapter, leadership is the underlying and distinguishing thread for top-performing senior-level executives. The following are guidelines from Murray Martin and Kenneth Chenault on becoming an industry leader.

MARTIN'S COACHING TIPS

- Remarkable leaders are open to honest assessment of their own strengths and gaps and use this information to develop themselves and to develop the organization around them.
- Be curious about the immediate and larger world around you. You must have peripheral vision and be aware of all aspects of your environment.
- Your written and verbal skills are a critical part of your personal brand. They provide a window into your judgment, your intellectual curiosity, and how you think. They are the basis on which others form their impression of you. It is extremely important to develop these skills for both one-on-one and larger group interactions.

CHENAULT'S COACHING TIPS

"It's not the strongest, most intelligent who survive, but those most adaptive to change," explained Kenneth Chenault in a recent lecture with students at the Wharton School of Business. He also provided his personal insights on the six key traits that serve as the foundation of a true leader:

1. **Act with integrity.** Many people construe integrity to mean being honest. That's a piece of it, but it's really about being *consistent* in words and actions.
2. **Act with courage.** To me, it's not personal. I want you to argue with me. It requires courage to offer a different perspective and challenge current or popular views. Chenault cites the Enron collapse as an example of what can happen when leadership lacks courage: "People saw things happening but didn't have the courage to speak out."

3. **Be a team player.** Don't confuse being a team player with being nice, he explains. "There can be nice people who are bad team players—people who don't engage in confrontation when that's really what's required. . . . I look at whether the person *helps* the team."

4. **Focus on execution.** "Today, people are more focused on IQ, but executional quotient, EQ, is just as important. If a person has a match of IQ and EQ, he has incredible personal commitment and can be an incredible force. Disparity between IQ and EQ means that person is just focused on himself."

5. **Be a developer of people.** "I judge the success of a leader by the success of the people who are the followership."

6. **Be proactive.** "At the end of the day it's important to take action and make things happen."

7

Be More Prepared Than Everyone Else

Because Minorities Need to Work Harder to Get Ahead

Luck is what happens when preparation meets opportunity.
—*Seneca, philosopher*

The deaths of two successive McDonald's CEOs and the resignation of a CFO moved Donald Thompson quickly from executive vice president of Global Innovation Orchestration in 2003 to executive vice president and chief operations officer of U.S. business and, in 2006, president of McDonald's USA. When he first got the call from a recruiter in 1990 to consider joining the company, he confused it with the aerospace manufacturer McDonnell Douglas. Thompson, who holds only a bachelor's in electrical engineering from Purdue University, flatly declined the offer. "You got the wrong guy, because I'm not flipping hamburgers for anybody," he explained in an interview with *Black Enterprise* magazine.

Thompson eventually did join the engineering department at the fast food giant, but realized that there would be little growth opportunity in that area. A company senior VP who became Thompson's mentor helped him transition into operations three years later, to learn that side of the business, where he became the director of strategic planning and quality management. Thompson was not quite familiar with the company's particular business issues, but he was talented at problem-solving and used that skill to anchor his performance. In the meantime, his mentor suggested he enroll in a development program to gain restaurant experience. In it Thompson performed every menial task possible. Yes, he did end up flipping burgers, but his experience in engineering, in operations, and now in the restaurant itself prepared Thompson not only to perform functional duties extremely well but to become an innovator at the company as well. Not only did he become intimately familiar with the demands of running a business internally, he was also well acquainted with the market forces and consumer attitudes that could impact their brand. Thompson has continuously proved his strategic genius at every level—even internationally. He has continuously been prepared to handle every challenge—and opportunity.

Be prepared. It seems like the most basic advice one could offer a minority manger—so elementary, it need not be discussed. But it may indeed be so basic that its importance is taken for granted. Preparation, however, in today's fast-paced competitive climate, is a fundamental and vital function of corporate success. And it often means being equipped to handle not only your present job requirements but internal and external challenges, transitions, and opportunities. It means being ready for the best, the worst, and the most untimely circumstances. Because so much business is conducted in environments outside of the office, you need to be socially equipped to talk about more than just business. For minority managers, being prepared also means being mentally ready to challenge and in some cases ignore stereotypical expectations of your talent, work ethic, and capabilities. When you move from middle to senior management, a very different level of preparation is required.

INSTILLED FROM CHILDHOOD

As a child coming of age during the civil rights movement of the 1960s, I attended a segregated public school in Cleveland, Ohio. Charles Dickens Elementary School was a typical school filled with black children from poor to lower-middle-class families. It was a school where our teachers cared, our parents were active in the Parent Teacher Association, and as students we were very competitive with one another. There was one event, however, during my fifth-grade year that forever changed my life.

As part of an "enrichment" program for gifted children, fifth- and sixth-graders shared a homeroom instructor whose purpose was to teach students additional skills to better prepare us for junior high school. In most cases, this meant a few extra homework assignments or an extra book report each month. My teacher, Ms. Carol Caputo, however, had something more in mind. Each week she demanded that each of us prepare a two-to-three-minute "short talk" on anything we read in the newspaper that week. We were to prepare our message on three-by-five index cards, in outline format, and stand and deliver our talk in front of our other classmates in perfect English.

While it was somewhat challenging at first, over time most students enjoyed and even looked forward to these "daily talks," as she called them. Some parents felt she had overstepped her boundaries, and she was brought before the PTA board. One by one several parents complained that this exercise was excessive, as the frequency encouraged anxiety in the children who were embarrassed or made nervous by public speaking.

Unmoved, Ms. Caputo addressed the audience: "Our children are growing up in a different time than most of you grew up. They will inherit a different world with far more options than many of you had. They will not be able to take advantage of those opportunities if they are not prepared. Prepared to think for themselves, interpret facts for themselves, and express themselves. Their futures are much brighter than we may realize today, and I want them to be prepared for whatever that future holds. They will be competing with children who are prepared, and will need to be more prepared to succeed." After her comments, many of the parents who had previously complained, many of whom worked in the steel mills or the automotive industries, gave her a rousing round of applause—and their full support.

Ms. Caputo realized in the 1960s that as little black children who would enter the workforce in the 1970s and '80s, we had to come to terms with the fact that, right, wrong, or indifferent, we had to be more prepared than our majority counterparts to succeed. She also understood that we were moving from an industrial economy to a service economy and that we had to be prepared for this new paradigm.

TODAY'S REALITY

To be honest, it is possible to have a career in a corporate company as an average worker—a C player. In fact, if you were to divide the workplace into A, B, and C employees, I would argue that A players represent 10 percent, and B players account for 25 percent, with the other 65 percent being C players or below. The C player is typically the person who does just what the job requires, no more and no less. The C player rarely takes the time to further her learning with an advanced degree or executive training courses to help improve her knowledge base, strengthen a skill, or enhance her leadership abilities. Nor will you find the average C player involved in developing and bolstering the necessary relationships, internally or externally, needed to enhance her visibility in the company as well as the industry. As a result, you will almost never find a C player in a C-suite position.

Minorities know they cannot afford to operate at the C level. As many of us were taught growing up, "You have to be twice as good!" To a young child, a student, and even a new entrant to the workforce, such advice might have felt burdensome. But many successful C-suite professionals will tell you that working twice as hard prepared them for the opportunities that ushered them to the top of their game. You must be committed to being prepared at all times! If you're not, I suggest you brush up your résumé and practice your interviewing skills, because minority C players are often the first to be laid off, downsized, right-sized, and/or fired when their company faces difficult times.

YOU CAN NEVER *NOT* BE PREPARED

I recently met with a dozen or so of the many college interns Pitney Bowes hires each and every year from the InRoads, a college intern program focused on preparing and placing minority students in corporate companies. To enhance their experience, we hold frequent executive roundtables where students get the opportunity to learn about business objectives and strategies directly from senior executives in the company.

On this particular occasion, one young Latino gentleman asked me this question: "Now that you are president, is it necessary for you to still work and prepare as hard as you did when you were just starting out?" He reasoned that, given how hard it must have been to get to this position, it should be much easier to stay there. He was surprised to learn that as president, I have to work even harder than before! The higher up you move in an organization, the more responsibility you have in managing and directing employees and other resources, and the more you are accountable for successes, failures, and driving results.

For example, I am required to prepare a quarterly presentation for our Senior Management Committee, covering my organization's previous quarter's performance and expectations for the next eight quarters. The meeting is only an hour long, but I prepare for weeks in advance for that meeting, not only covering the points of business but examining every ramification of those points. I prepare not just for questions but for criticisms, possible perceived flaws, and risk-averse assessments. Not being prepared to handle any possible contentions in such a meeting would signal that I was unable to manage my position.

✦ Calvin's Story:
The Price of Not Being Prepared

Here's another example: I recently needed to fill a VP position, and interviewed several candidates. I was amazed at how many minority candidates didn't come prepared to their interview with a thirty/ sixty/ninety-day plan outlining their intentions for the position should they be given the job. No one presented a vision of how he would hit the ground running and make an impact. But their white counterparts *did* come with those plans.

I'm a firm believer in giving feedback, and so after we made our selection, I explained to some of the minority managers why they didn't get the position. One manager, named Calvin, told me that because of his solid track record and his fifteen-year history with the company, he believed he didn't need to prepare further for that interview. He was wrong. Your track record may get you an interview at the table, but it doesn't guarantee you a seat. At this level the stakes are higher, the competition is stiffer, and the margin for error almost nonexistent. You have to be prepared professionally, strategically, personally, and mentally for every encounter with clients, customers, senior managers, and peers. It takes just one poor board presentation because you aren't prepared, or one executive committee meeting where you don't have all the facts, to end your career—particularly in fiercely competitive environments where top spots are coveted, in environments where they believe you are just a diversity hire. There are colleagues waiting for you to fall short, colleagues who are preparing to take your spot.

COACHING TIPS

The following are several tips emphasizing the importance of preparedness:

Be prepared by having your day planned in advance. As a rule, most successful executives interviewed on this subject stated that they took the time each evening to prepare for the next business day. For some, that meant even readying their wardrobe the night before. The primary reason: given their extremely hectic schedules, preparing the evening before allowed them to be mentally ready for the expectations of the day ahead. As a result, they would often uncover ways to be more efficient in their tasks, assignments, or meetings. These were some of the benefits:

• Prereading any information to be covered during a meeting allowed them to go in with familiarity with the subject to be discussed. Preparing the night before gave them the opportunity not only to write down questions and comments but to really give them adequate thought. If they had not prepared in advance, their effectiveness would have been greatly diminished, as they would have to process information without the benefit of forethought, and as a result might overlook or forget important questions until after the call or meeting was over.

• By reviewing the day in advance, they were able to set aside time for returning important calls, reading and responding to e-mail, creating a to-do list, and beginning the day more organized. When they did not do so, these executives stated that they often felt disorganized, were delinquent in reading and replying to e-mail, and were less effective overall.

Be prepared for internal meetings and presentations. From a visibility perspective, internal meetings and presentations are an ideal time to display your talents—or, if you're unprepared, the lack thereof. This is even more critical for minorities, whose actions are typically viewed under a microscope. Your stock will rise or fall quickly, depending on how well you are perceived during such meetings. I cannot tell you how many career opportunities have been created because a senior executive was impressed with how well someone performed during a meeting or while giving a presentation.

Always master the material. Nothing is more impressive than to have complete control of the facts in a meeting. The person who knows and understands the material and has control of the facts comes across as confident, credible, and fully engaged in the details of the business.

• Take the time required to thoroughly review all relevant meeting materials prior to the meeting, making sure the materials support the agenda.

• Do outside research via the Internet, periodicals, industry publications, and so on that will provide you with more insight into the subject at hand.

• Identify three to five key observations or points you would like to make during the meeting.

Rehearse, rehearse, then rehearse some more. For most people, giving a presentation or speaking in public is already a challenging proposition. To do this without rehearsing can make an already stressful situation downright miserable and possibly embarrassing. In my career I have observed key executives deliver flawless, polished presentations that left their audience totally impressed. When I inquired as to how they seemed to be so at ease in front of their audience, they all gave the same answer: "Lots of rehearsing." Further discussions revealed that many would stand in front of a mirror or family members and deliver their presentation over and over until they were comfortable. Then they would actually rehearse in their minds and anticipate questions from the audience and have answers prepared in advance. If public speaking is a real problem for you, consider joining Toastmasters International or take a course in public speaking. It will be one of the best investments you can make.

Always have an intelligent, thoughtful question to ask. I will never forget an event that happened early in my management career. Two brand-new hires, one a minority male and the other a white male, were invited to participate in our monthly leaders' meeting. Both men sat during the two-hour meeting without saying a word. Most likely they were content just to observe and take meaningful notes. What was eye-opening to me was the remarks made by my peers at the conclusion of the meeting. When commenting on the young white executive, they observed, "Didn't Brad really seem engaged during the meeting? It's like he soaked in every word." When speaking of the minority gentleman, however, their observation was very different: "It seemed like James was lost during the meeting," one said. "He just didn't seem to follow the discussion." Instantly, I reminded them that neither gentleman had said a word during the meeting, and that both took notes on key points. This further reinforced that there can be a double standard for minorities even regarding *not* speaking in a meeting!

I learned early in my career the value of always asking at least one meaningful, insightful question during business meetings. This demonstrates not only that you are actively listening and are engaged in the discussion but that you have interpreted the key points, and have serious thought leadership to add to the discussion.

Be prepared for performance appraisals and internal job interviews. One of the areas that we tend to underestimate is how important it is to prepare for annual performance reviews and internal job interviews within our current companies. In the case of annual performance appraisals, it is important that you take time to document your performance against the goals and objectives assigned to you earlier in the year by your manager. Ideally, you can measure your activities, accomplishments, and results against these targets to make your case for the highest performance rating possible. Furthermore, I strongly suggest that, since most managers dread having to write year-end appraisals, you take the liberty to write your own appraisal and share it with your manager. This will accomplish two things. First, you will help dictate the tone and content of your appraisal by giving your manager a predetermined script that will allow her to make modifications and add her content to your written document. Second, it gives you the opportunity to highlight those accomplishments that your manager may or may not be aware of, and thus may actually positively affect the comments from your manager.

Being ill prepared for internal job interviews is another luxury that minority professionals cannot afford. While conventional wisdom may dictate that because you are a known entity within your organization, you need less preparation, I would argue that just the opposite is true. Because you are already with the organization, it is quite possible that others have a perception of your abilities based upon what they have observed firsthand or have heard about you from others. Perhaps someone participated in a meeting with you, worked with you on a project, or simply sat next to you at a company function. The fact remains that a perception of you and your abilities has been created that can work either for or against you during an internal interview. While it may be impossible to know exactly what perceptions others may have of you in the organization, it is possible to use the interviewing process to set the record straight as to who you are, and what you bring to the table. In addition to making sure you have a complete understanding of what the requirements are for the position you are applying for, I suggest that you also come prepared to every internal interview with the following:

• **A list of the perceived challenges/opportunities that currently exist for whoever gets the position.** This will demonstrate to the interviewer your analytical skills and the fact that you have given serious thought to the role. To gain this information, you may have to have informal discussions with others familiar with the job, or insight into the previous performance of the department, territory, or team you will be leading. It could be that your sales territories need to be better aligned to take advantage of market opportunities. Or there may be gaps in your product line that you need to fill. Conceivably, you may need to remedy a morale issue that has led to a disengaged workforce. Whatever the challenge or opportunity, it is important that you at least discuss your thoughts as to what these may be.

• **A high-level thirty/sixty/ninety-day action plan on how to address these challenges and take advantage of the opportunities.** Every senior leader wants to know that she is dealing with a person of action! It's not enough to be able to identify areas of improvement and opportunity. You must show that you have a plan to meet these head-on. This plan should detail at a high level what actions you would take during your first thirty days on the job, your next thirty days on the job, and what you expect to accomplish after having been in the role your first ninety days. While admittedly this plan will need to be modified as you learn more about the role, it demonstrates to the interviewer that you have a plan, and that you think strategically. In his book *The First 90 Days*, Michael Watkins offers critical success strategies for new leaders at all levels.

• **Examples of how your previous experience makes you uniquely qualified for this role.** Once you understand what the job requirements and qualifications are, it is important that you *sell* the interviewer on how your background makes you the ideal candidate for the role. If the job requires you to grow revenues, cite examples from your past in which your efforts led to significant revenue growth. If the position requires you to improve profitability, come prepared to discuss actions you have taken to enhance profitability. Remember, an interview is nothing more than a selling opportunity, and you are both the salesperson and the product. Managers are always more comfortable hiring individuals with a proven track record of success in the key areas required in the new role. The more you can give tangible examples of previous success, the better your chances of landing the job!

Managers who have risen to the top understand the importance and power of always being prepared. You can never underestimate the power of being prepared, and the impact it can have on your career. Make sure that you make the investment in yourself to always put your best foot forward and never leave any doubt that at all times, you are prepared.

Never stop improving your knowledge base. Having a degree may be the requirement for certain management positions, but because market demands change so rapidly, it is important to continually update what you know. Of course it's important to keep abreast of industry trends by reading industry trade journals and attending professional conferences. Staying current may also require taking an executive training course. There are a variety of programs specially tailored for almost every type of business strategy that currently exists.

THE IMPORTANCE OF BEING MENTALLY, EMOTIONALLY, AND SPIRITUALLY PREPARED

When it comes to working in corporate environments, minorities face additional challenges in being prepared. In addition to the basics highlighted earlier in this chapter, minorities face challenges that will test their will, value systems, and patience, and even their own self-perception. These challenges can come in the form of an insensitive boss, stereotypes thrust upon them by colleagues and clients, and the internal doubts that everyone wrestles with from time to time. It can come from having your competence questioned for no other reason than the color of your skin or the neighborhood you grew up in.

"As minorities we tend to start out behind the eight ball because of the conditioning of the American culture which tends to still feel that we are not as intelligent, equipped, or good," offers author and emotional wellness expert Dr. Lawana Gladney. "Growing up I was taught that you have to be better than average in order to prove your worth. Going into a situation with that thought alone speaks to the importance of being emotionally prepared and keeping your emotions in check."

Minorities can face unique challenges from white counterparts, and even from other minorities who feel threatened by their success. If they are not dealt with properly, the stresses brought on by these challenges can have a devastating impact on a minority manager's effectiveness.

It can be easy for nonminorities to dismiss these challenges and minimize their impact. Certain experiences that minorities face will never be fully understood or appreciated by their majority counterparts. Likewise, it is important that minorities understand and react appropriately to these challenges so they do not inadvertently sabotage themselves. You have to be prepared mentally, emotionally, and spiritually for the inevitable situations you will face.

Minorities Must Be Mentally Prepared

✦ *"You CAN'T Be the Boss!"*

Many times in my own career, I have dealt with the frustration of being a minority executive in a majority world. Not too long ago, I went with one of my vice presidents and his director to visit a client for a quarterly business review. It was the first such meeting we had had with this client, and we were all very anxious to discuss our great results in working for the client the previous quarter. As we entered the room, we decided to delay introductions until after we had time to build rapport. As my director, who happened to be an older white gentleman, began to review the agenda, I noticed that all of the client's attention was on my VP, who was also an older white male. Nearly all conversation was directed at my VP, and the client even told him how well "his" team had been performing. As we moved on to doing introductions, the director stated how pleased he was to have his president take part in the meeting. Immediately, all eyes went to my VP. They naturally assumed that there was no way I was the president! It was beyond satisfying to see the look on their faces once I began to thank them for their business, and it was clear to them that, in fact, the bald-headed black guy was the boss!

If this were an isolated event, it could be viewed as an accident. Unfortunately, it happens more often than I'd like to admit or experience. Earlier in my career I would have let such a situation frustrate me, or worse yet, cause me to react inappropriately. However, over time I have become mentally prepared to handle such situations.

An Executive Coach May Be the Answer

To be completely honest, I did not learn to handle such situations on my own. Over the course of my career I have had the good fortune to work for companies who provided me with executive coaches. Typically, companies hire these external coaches to help high-potential executives overcome shortcomings that may be hindering their professional growth. These shortcomings can range from executives who have trouble building followership to issues around interpersonal communications and a host of other areas that may be creating blind spots for the executive. In my case, I was having challenges with being the "only minority in the room," a condition Dr. Wilbert R. Sykes refers to as the "unique minority of one (UMO)" syndrome, which manifested itself in the form of unnecessary confrontation to make certain I was not being overlooked. After interviewing several coaches, I settled on Sykes, chairman and CEO of the TriSource Group. TriSource is an executive coaching and partnership consultation organization that works with professional organizations, corporations, and their senior executives and management teams to function more effectively, individually and as a team.

In working with me, Sykes helped me cut to the core of my inability to be as mentally prepared as I should. Most nonminorities have made judgments about me based on my discernible attributes, namely how I look, dress, and speak, where I was born, and so on, coupled with the negative stereotypes they may have observed in the media. These judgments have usually been negative. Because many of these same individuals reacted to me negatively without knowing me or having any insight into my "inner world," my thoughts, feelings, beliefs, ambitions, ideals, and values, it created a resentment factor in me. As a result, whenever I found myself being the "only minority in the room," I automatically *assumed* that these majority individuals were prejudging me negatively, and set out to display to them that I was not who they saw on the latest episode of *Cops*. The downside of my behavior was that I was actually alienating myself, rather than creating an environment conducive to effective team building.

How to Prepare Mentally If You Are a "Unique Minority of One"

How should unique minorities of one (UMOs) prepare themselves, knowing that most other individuals will largely relate to them in terms of their discernible attributes? Dr. Sykes offers the following advice:

1. UMOs should know that people who do not like them might, on the other hand, admire things about them if they knew them better.
2. Therefore people's judgments, based on their knowledge of discernible attributes, will be incomplete and shouldn't be taken as applying to the totality of who we are or shouldn't be reacted to as if those judgments did.
3. UMOs should also know that people who know little of us may take their little knowledge and "make up" the rest of us to accord with their preconceived notions.
4. UMOs should know that such an elaboration of who someone is, based on minimal knowledge of discernible attributes, is something that we are all guilty of doing. (Nature isn't the only assessor that abhors a vacuum!)
5. UMOs should know that most of the behavior that people find so surprising in other people is brought about because of *unfounded assessments* of who those other people were in the first place.
6. UMOs should know that physical appearance, or behavior under a public spotlight, does not say very much about a person's inner world.

7. UMOs should know that the discernible attributes that they control in presenting themselves to the world at large are *stimuli,* and that the world's reactions to them and those attributes are *effects.*

8. UMOs should know that the description of us from one observer based on our discernible attributes, when passed on to another person, may be taken by that other person as accurate and predictive.

9. UMOs should caution themselves about evaluating what they know of others if the UMO's information base doesn't warrant much certainty of accuracy.

10. UMOs should know that other people are often not as aware of or sensitive to the fact that their knowledge and understanding are often incomplete and necessarily inaccurate. They believe in their "knowledge," and we will all be victimized by this misapprehension.

"All of the above understandings, if applied, make us more mature in our thinking about others and less sensitive about their misperceptions and misunderstandings of who we are," says Dr. Sykes.

Minorities Must Be Emotionally Prepared

How often have you heard the phrases, "She's too emotional," "He has a chip on his shoulder," "Why is she so sensitive?," or "He always seems to be so distrustful"? More than likely, it is possible that these phrases have been uttered about you by majority professionals you work with. This is partly because they have bought into the negative stereotypes of the "angry black woman" or the "hot Latin temper" that proliferate in movies and television. Additionally, many who have not spent much time with minorities tend to paint all minorities with the same brush.

However, I would argue that, in part, people base these comments and beliefs on what they observe when a minority who has tried to hide or ignore his emotions finally blows his top! You see, for many minorities, a coping mechanism, necessary in order to coexist and avoid a "troublemaker" label, is to avoid showing emotion. The problem is that we are emotional creatures, and having emotions is not wrong. The issue becomes, how do we handle these emotions? Inevitably, as a minority you will be confronted with situations that will challenge you emotionally. A coworker stabs you in the back. A boss gives you an unfair rating. A promised promotion is given to another. These are all events that can't help but trigger an emotional response, and to deal with them you must be emotionally prepared.

✦ Chuck's Emotional Struggle: "Thank God for C.S.I."

A terrific example of the need to be emotionally prepared comes from a dear friend of mine, Chuck. Chuck had just been hired as the VP of sales for the financial services practice of a consulting firm. Part of his responsibility was to work with Edward, the firm's VP of operations, to make sure that every engagement was sold and implemented smoothly. As a result, they typically went on joint calls together to visit prospects and clients, and worked hand in hand in determining the terms and conditions of contracts with clients.

Because Chuck was new to financial services, but not new to sales, he decided to spend the first thirty days getting acquainted with industry terms, challenges, and opportunities so that he could speak intelligently with clients, before making any calls with Edward, and explained as much to him. Within a matter of two weeks Chuck was informed by his boss that Edward had been complaining that Chuck was not willing to visit clients. Chuck gave his rationale to his boss, who understood, and assured him that within a few weeks he would be more visible with clients. Edward's actions left a bitter taste in Chuck's mouth, but he decided not to confront Edward about it. Roughly a month later, during a meeting with his boss, Chuck was asked how things were going between him and Edward. Chuck answered, "Fine," but was curious as to the reason for the question. His boss suggested that perhaps he and Edward should go to breakfast and have a heart-to-heart conversation, because Edward had just shared with him that he felt Chuck was not qualified for the VP role.

That afternoon, Chuck called me to vent. In his mind, Edward was "jeopardizing his ability to provide for his family," and Chuck had had enough! His thoughts ranged from physically assaulting Edward himself to hiring someone to "take him out." Chuck declared the only thing that kept him from doing the latter was an episode of the television show *C.S.I. (Crime Scene Investigation)* that convinced him he would eventually get caught. After he calmed down, I assured him that his first impulse was just as irrational, but that emotionally he had every right to be upset. After I convinced him to meet with Edward and rationally voice his displeasure, Chuck in fact did meet with him. After a brief, heated discussion, in which Chuck learned that Edward had been one of the internal candidates who didn't get the VP of sales job, the two men committed to working on their relationship. However, had Chuck let his emotions get the best of him, the outcome could have been vastly more negative.

What Is It to Be Emotionally Prepared?

Emotion can be hard to manage in the workplace because of all the stereotypes, cultural biases, and preconceived notions about race and gender that everyone brings to the office. Minorities are obviously at a disadvantage—after all, they are in the minority—and proving yourself and your worth to an organization, as we have learned, requires more than just being good at your job. A huge part of maintaining your sanity in corporate America is moving past what you believe others think of you and your abilities—as well as what power or influence they have over your possible success at the company. Those feelings of insecurity, Dr. Gladney explains, are why minorities tend to have trust issues with the majority culture. "We think they have a hidden agenda. We know that typically [they] tend to feel uncomfortable in our presence and that puts us in position to make others feel comfortable with us. That alone adds to the difficulty of achieving emotional wellness."

But if trust issues are causing you to be guarded, fearful, and even insular, such behavior will perpetuate a cycle of misjudgments on both sides. In order to manage emotional stresses, Dr. Gladney offers some basic advice: "Know who you are [and] stay true to yourself." But she also advises against ignoring your emotions. Ignoring or suppressing how they feel is the reason many explode when they believe they have been pushed or challenged too far. Instead, she suggests taking time to think and examine problems logically before reacting, and addressing issues as they arise.

Minorities Must Be Spiritually Prepared

In my experience talking to many successful minorities during my career, almost all understood and agreed with the idea of being both mentally and emotionally prepared for the challenges of working in business. Because of our unique backgrounds and experiences, minorities have the added challenge of creating a thick outer shell to avoid being derailed by the actions and misperceptions of those who are afraid of our discernible differences. However, when I talk with many of those who have reached the highest level of leadership, they claim that one more level of preparedness is required for the journey: being spiritually prepared.

Regardless of their religious background, beliefs, or denominations, these executives (myself included) all claim to have reached a point of frustration and disappointment at some point in their careers that forced them to look inward for "divine guidance" in order to overcome the obstacles in their path. Mere intelligence, skill, networking, and their relationships were not enough to sustain them during these difficult days.

A Spiritual Leader's Perspective

To better illustrate the concept of being spiritually prepared, I called upon the Reverend W. Darin Moore, senior pastor at Greater Centennial AME Zion Church, one of the largest AME Zion congregations in the United States, located in Mount Vernon, New York. Pastor Moore, whose congregation consists of members from all walks of life, has on many occasions been called upon to offer leadership advice and council to the many doctors, lawyers, business executives, and political leaders who look to him for spiritual guidance. One of his most insightful lessons on being spiritually prepared is wrapped up in the concept of the need for leaders to be VIPs. Below Pastor Moore offers insight into this concept:

Preparation is derived from two Latin words that, when combined, mean "to make ready before time." It is more than simply having a plan, as important as that is. It is about having laid the mental and spiritual foundations necessary for success in life. History is replete with intelligent and gifted individuals who lacked the internal qualifications requisite to successfully seize the moment.

Those who are prepared to take advantage of opportunities when they arise are what I call VIPs. A VIP is a person who possesses the *vision, integrity,* and *perseverance* to emerge as a leader in any situation. These are the dynamic individuals throughout history who have risen to prominence and proved to be effective agents of transformation in all areas of life.

✦ *Joseph's Story:*
From the Pit to the Palace

One example of a VIP is the biblical character of Joseph. He was raised in a Hebrew home as the youngest of twelve brothers, in relative obscurity, and yet rose to be the CEO of Egypt, the most powerful nation in his day. His is a story of overcoming discrimination and hostility to transform a society and save his own family. When reviewing Joseph's journey from the pit to the palace, one is gripped by the overarching sense of vision, integrity, and perseverance that shaped his destiny and that of his people.

THE VIPs OF LEADERSHIP

1. Vision. Vision is the ability to see beyond what is, to what can be. Every great leader has been able to look beyond the limitations of their present realities and envision the potential for a better future, be it Martin Luther King Jr., Marcus Garvey, Madame C. J. Walker, or Dr. Mark Dean, the IBM vice president who holds three of the nine original patents on which all personal computers are based. Each of these great African Americans refused to accept the status quo as the limitation, but rather viewed it as a starting point to move into a greater reality.

Joseph incurred the animosity of his brothers because of his ability to dream (or envision). They were jealous of the reward that came with this exceptional ability, a coat of many colors, but did not recognize the enormous responsibility incumbent on those with vision and the wonderful opportunities for all to benefit from it. Joseph had to learn, often through difficult experiences, how to articulate his vision and formulate appropriate plans for successful implementation.

Vision is both a gift that is bestowed and a skill to be refined. Often gifted people fail to do the hard work and develop the discipline necessary to sharpen their visionary skills, while skilled managers miss the opportunities to cultivate their inherent gifts to envision beyond the daily routines of their jobs. It is essential that every leader feed his spirit by exercising his "faith muscle." Daily times of prayer or meditation are vital to developing vision. It is by connecting with the power of the Divine that we are able to envision opportunities beyond the ordinary. Much as it is impossible to pick up an FM radio station with an AM receiver, one cannot develop the capacity to envision a great future when trapped in the mundane—it's the wrong frequency. A healthy spiritual life is the vital catalyst for vision.

2. Integrity. Integrity has to do with internal and external consistency. In other words, we are who we claim to be, or in the words of Barry White, "we practice what we preach." Anyone can wear the mask of ethics for a limited time, during an interview, for a retreat, or in front of a supervisor, but eventually who we really are as a person will emerge. Ethics must not just be a bullet in a PowerPoint presentation; it must be an integral part of who we are.

Joseph was enticed into a potentially compromising position when the wife of his immediate supervisor tested his integrity. Rather than succumbing to her advances and jeopardizing his future advancement, he maintained his credibility by avoiding all unethical behavior. As a result of his moral convictions, he experienced temporary persecution, but ultimately he was vindicated and his reputation for honesty was well established.

All leaders are confronted with difficult choices, but once you have made the decision to be a person of integrity, it puts all your subsequent choices in the right perspective. Ultimately, people do not follow leaders they cannot trust, and if people do not follow, then you cease to be a leader. It's that simple; integrity is nonnegotiable when it comes to being an effective leader. Because Joseph had demonstrated his trustworthiness in personal affairs, he was entrusted with major corporate responsibilities.

3. Perseverance. *"Humpty Dumpty sat on a wall. Humpty Dumpty had a great fall. All the king's horses and all the king's men couldn't put Humpty together again."* Even as a child, something bothered me about that nursery rhyme. What was an egg doing sitting up on a wall? He wasn't prepared to handle high places. Under stress, he cracked too easily. Until he was better prepared, he would have been safer at a lower level. He could have benefited from prior experience in some hot water.

Effective leaders have encountered some difficulties in life and in their careers and persevered. It's a tenet of the Christian faith that testifies that our trials make us strong. While no one enjoys such challenges while they are in the midst of them, upon reflection they provide invaluable experience and preparation for the greater challenges that come with greater responsibilities. Rejections teach you to be better prepared for the next interview; betrayals teach you to be warier about putting your trust in unproven people; setbacks force you to consider alternative solutions and show you better options for success. The only difference between those who overcome and those who quit is that the overcomer persevered in the face of adversity.

Joseph experienced the envy and subsequent betrayal of his brothers; he was thrown into a pit and then sold into slavery. He would later be falsely accused and forced to serve time in prison, but rather than becoming bitter and giving up, he persevered. As a result, he was promoted to oversee all the financial and administrative affairs of Egypt. Joseph's life is a marvelous example of how we can be overlooked and discriminated against, yet with the right attitude we have a promotion in our future. In fact, for Joseph, it was the lessons learned in having survived the pit and having endured the prison that prepared him to be able to successfully handle the responsibilities of the palace.

COACHING TIP

It is important to understand that for minorities, being prepared is not an option; it is an imperative. Furthermore, your idea of "prepared" must expand beyond the obvious activities required to perform the given role. To truly be a successful leader, you must take a holistic approach to preparedness that includes being mentally, emotionally, and spiritually prepared as well.

8

Overcoming Gender Bias

The Double Whammy
Facing Minority Women

"I think *The Godfather* is one of the best movies and books written on business," said Renetta McCann during a 2003 interview for *Black Enterprise* magazine, where she was being honored as Corporate Executive of the Year. "Of course it's about the mob, but if you go back and look at Don Corleone, he surrounded himself with good advisors. He always knew who his opponents were. He worked on quid pro quo—so he did things for people and they did things for him. He never made a move before his time and he was always in control of himself. He was always mad at Sonny," the CEO of Starcom MediaVest Group continued, "because Sonny could never control himself, and that's why Sonny ended up dead."

McCann's comparison of corporate America to the mob may be extreme—even dramatic—but it is very accurate. The success of one who began her career in a client services media training program and rose to head one of the world's largest advertising companies has been rooted in hard work and integrity, but executed with a firm understanding of what it really takes to win at the corporate level. That's where most women lose their footing—underestimating the importance of fully engaging in the game.

As we have detailed throughout this book, moving through the ranks of corporate America requires much more than acquiring the right degrees and working hard. It demands a plan—one for every unique situation you encounter as it relates to that company's culture. The "rules of the Godfather" are the rules of business as it applies to corporate strategy—particularly for women.

He surrounded himself with good advisors. In corporate-speak, these are an employee's mentors and sponsors. We will devote an entire chapter to the importance of such advisors. These are often senior-level executives inside and outside of an organization who not only offer advice and guidance on career direction but clue employees into the unspoken rules of engagement in a company and industry as well as inspiring confidence, keeping their mentees focused, and making recommendations on their behalf. Having influential mentors and sponsors is the most important element of gaining recognition and promotions within a company. A 2003 Catalyst report entitled *Women in US Corporate Leadership* revealed that the number-one barrier for women overall was lack of significant general management or line experience. Mentors and sponsors will suggest that an employee take specific assignments, join a special task force, or even restructure her career goals to help a woman best position herself for the necessary growth and development within the company. A 2004 Catalyst report focusing on African American managers revealed that their most common barrier to success was "not having an influential sponsor/mentor."

He knew his opponents. Opponents to employees in corporate America can include actual competitive challengers as well as real and/or perceived barriers. Understanding the culture of your company will help you decipher all of these components, and mentors are key decoders. When you truly understand how your company functions—not just how it does business, but the underlying elements and idiosyncrasies that drive business decisions—then you are able to develop the strongest alliances and strategies for your success.

He worked on quid pro quo. This is the development of your network. The first rule of networking is establishing relationships where you are helpful to those from whom you also seek assistance. Your network should be developed on several levels, which means you should be involved in a variety of activities and events inside and outside of your organization. Inside, it might mean joining coworkers for a couple of drinks after work, or joining the company's softball team, or attending "optional" holiday events. Through these gatherings, you should develop a cadre of internal colleagues with whom you have mutually beneficial relationships—relationships outside of a mentor or sponsor.

Outside of your company, becoming active in industry organizations will help you strengthen your industry contacts—professionals you are able to call on for tactical advice, referrals, and general information. Developing strong networks is an area where women and minorities regularly fall short—because it takes work.

Networks can't happen unless you decide to step outside of your comfort zone to develop them. Women are often so focused on getting the work done that they usually don't make time for lunches, dinners, conferences, and/or joining industry organizations where these relationships are developed and solidified. Minority women also tend to be more insular about their relationships in the workplace. They tend not to share personal information with coworkers, which can create a negative perception and close off relationships that could eventually be helpful to their career. As a result, minority women find themselves outside the benefit of informal networks that develop naturally for white men and women.

He never made a move before his time. This rule speaks to the importance of preparation, and of understanding what may be required before "your time" comes. In today's environment, women not only have to be functionally prepared to handle an opportunity, they have to be prepared for changes in company structure, technology, overall industry structure, and a variety of other elements that could alter the nature of their strategy.

✦ *Michelle's Story*

Michelle Greene was on assignment in Sweden when she learned that her director would soon be moved into a new role. He and Michelle believed that she was an obvious choice to succeed him as director of global IT for Sony Ericsson Mobile Communications, but selecting Greene was not as obvious to her peers and some outsiders—including the company's CIO. "Sony Ericsson is a very young company, and nothing stands still for very long, so just when I thought I was settled, a new challenge was set for me," she explains. "The group was highly technical and responsible for a budget of EUR12,000,000. My background was not predominantly technical, and I had never managed a large budget. I was [also] a relative newcomer to the group. Others were far better qualified on the technical front and had been in the group since the beginning and clearly felt they would be the natural successors."

But Greene's manager had confidence in her beyond her technical shortcomings. He saw her as a solid leader, someone who was always able to enlist the support and backing of the team. He also saw Greene as someone who was able to always perform beyond the expectations of the group, which was important, as this organization was expanding their company globally. "Mentors and sponsors have played a key role in my success by providing endless encouragement and support," she notes. "Most importantly, they were willing to have the tough discussions with me regarding areas where I needed to develop or make improvements." Those were the areas she focused on and developed, and she was promoted to director. Today she is director of business infrastructure within the corporate IT organization, a position that has expanded four times in size and covers several countries throughout the world in Asia, Europe, and the United States.

"The lesson learned is that I can handle any challenge that is set for me as long as the goals and objectives are understood. It is also important to surround yourself with people that will not only have a positive impact on your life but will also be willing to let you know when the time has come for you to move forward."

• • •

Successfully playing out the "rules of the Godfather" means adhering to each of the tenets strategically—and impersonally—without sentiment. Remember Renetta's analogy: "That's why Sonny ended up dead." He was too emotional—a trait that is also often strongly associated with women. Emotion in the workplace is often seen as a sign of weakness. As a result, many women work extremely hard at excising any of their feminine traits in a business environment.

What many don't realize is that there are many positive things about being and acting like a woman that benefit the organization.

+ *Jenny's Story*

When Jenny Alonzo got the call about an opportunity to become director of promotions for a hot new talk show in the fall of 1992, she wasted no time considering whether to interview for the position. "It was the perfect job," she says. Alonzo at the time was also married and a new mother, and she and her husband had a weekday routine that worked: the two would drive the baby to Jenny's mom, and then leave from there and take public transportation to their respective jobs in New York City. In the evening, they would meet to pick up the baby and then drive home from her mother's house.

On the evening of the interview, Alonzo told her husband that she would be a little later than usual. The meeting would begin at 6:00 p.m., and she estimated that she would be done by 7:30. The interview was stellar. The gentleman with whom she interviewed was so impressed, he wanted Alonzo to meet his boss, a significant player in the organization. It was now 7:15.

They waited for the gentleman to arrive and engaged in another successful meeting. Both were certain that Alonzo was the best person for the job and wanted to show her the studio. It was now 8:15, and Alonzo was panicked. "It was back in 1992, when not everyone had a cell phone. I didn't have one," she explains. "I knew my husband and mother were probably wondering what happened, but I didn't feel confident enough to excuse myself from these two men and find a phone to make the call. They wanted to talk next steps, and in my mind, excusing myself to say that I had to check in with my husband and child might show weakness on my part—having a child might communicate that I wouldn't be able to commit to this project."

By the time Alonzo finished with the tour, it was roughly 9:15. Alonzo had planned to take a taxi, but the gentlemen offered to call her a car service. Again, she didn't want to offend them in any way. After all, she felt that these two men held her fate. This was an important, career-impacting opportunity. She waited for the car, which arrived a half hour later. When she reached her mother's home, Jenny's mom was upset that she hadn't called to say she'd be late, and her husband and child had left. It was after 11:00 when Alonzo got home; her husband was furious. They got into such a serious argument, she feared for her marriage. She turned down the job offer.

It's a story that Alonzo retells often to young coworkers and young women she mentors. Out of that situation Alonzo learned one of her biggest and hardest lessons as she began her corporate climb in television, to eventually become senior vice president of multicultural strategies and initiatives for Lifetime Entertainment Services: she learned how crippling fear can be. Alonzo was twenty-six at the time, and didn't have a mentor. She also didn't have a lot of female role models as examples of how to manage clashing expectations at home and on the job. "Today I know that all I had to say was, 'Excuse me, gentlemen, I need to call home and check on my family, and let them know I'll be late.' Today, I know that being a married woman with children is not a weakness, but a situation I could have leveraged to show my variety of strengths."

Fortunately, the fact that women, simply by who they are, benefit an organization is becoming more widely discussed and accepted in corporate America.

EMOTION VERSUS PASSION

It was long believed that for a woman to excel in a male-dominated environment, she should act and behave like a man. In recent years, however, we have come to openly accept that men and women not only think differently, but will react and execute differently—and that traits inherent in a woman's behavior can actually be good for business. In fact, a *USA Today* article reported that in 2006, several of the five hundred largest publicly traded companies headed by women outperformed the Standard & Poor's 500 index.

Women tend to be more intuitive, which means they can be better forecasters of trends. They are more flexible, which means they can easily make adjustments in management styles. They are more nurturing, making them better attuned to the needs of their employees and better at developing talent within their company. Women tend to be better communicators, making them more responsive to giving and accepting feedback. Books like *Pitch Like a Girl: How a Woman Can Be Herself and Still Succeed*, by Ronna Lichtenberg (Rodale, 2005), actually break down management styles between men and women into pink and blue categories, with stark differences between the two. *Pink*, a business magazine for women, published an (August/September 2007) article on how women's brains are better wired for business. Their findings: "The corpus callosum [in the brain] is an information network that, in women, has more and different kinds of messages traveling in both directions, resulting in an increased ability to process many tasks at once. Men, on the other hand, tend to use the right hemisphere more, helping them to focus on problems involving spatial components."

Other interesting differences they found: "Women are as concerned about process as they are about outcomes; men are concerned primarily with outcomes. Women negotiate in a win/win manner; men negotiate in a win/lose manner. Women are interactive leaders; men are command-and-control leaders."

Women also tend to be more emotional, which is really just a distraction from your goals. Emotion should never be confused with passion. Passion is the exuberance that you bring to your work. Emotion is your attachment to the outcome of that work. Passion can bring great satisfaction. Emotion—even when it is well guarded and internalized—will bring despair, frustration, increased stress, and sometimes defeat. Emotion diverts your focus. When you are emotional, you lose sight of the issue, the problem, the job that has to be completed, and you begin concentrating on how offended, slighted, and angry someone else—who has no respect for your position or who is competing for your job—has made you. Not that you shouldn't address disrespectful behavior, but according to Renetta, you can't let anybody get into your head. "At this level, everybody's got an agenda and it's not always yours," she said. "A person who's a friend on Monday is a foe on Tuesday. I don't let anybody mess with my head."

BREAKING THROUGH THE CONCRETE CEILING

McCann and others among the highest-ranking women have undoubtedly mastered the rules of engagement and the concept, "It's business, not personal." But those women who continue to struggle to make inroads in corporate America are by no means imagining pressures. The 2003 Catalyst report *Women in US Corporate Leadership* identified several barriers to women's success in the workplace:

1. Lack of significant general management or line experience
2. Exclusion from informal networks
3. Stereotyping and preconceptions of women's roles and abilities
4. Failure of senior leadership to assume accountability for women's advancement
5. Commitment to personal or family responsibilities. (A 2005 Wharton Center for Leadership and Change study, *Back in the Game: Returning to Business*, reported that women who leave the workplace for personal or family responsibilities have an extremely hard time reentering the workforce. Respondents to the survey said that recruiters and employers often believed that they had lost skills and their ability to perform business tasks because of their absence.)

But in its 2004 study, Catalyst found that the proverbial "glass ceiling" that many women had found difficult to shatter is even more impenetrable for black women. According to *Advancing African-American Women in the Workplace: What Managers Need to Know*, the glass ceiling was a "cement ceiling" in their case. Black women have to deal not only with gender-based stereotypes but also with race-based stereotypes, which in many business environments can leave them outside of power circles.

✦ *Adriane's Story*

Earlier in her career, Adriane Brown, had been with her company for ten years, with a great track record, and was just returning from an educational leave during which she'd earned her MBA, sponsored by the company. The division to which she was returning was new, and she didn't know anyone. In fact, several other female coworkers warned Adriane that this was a tough division—one that "chews women up and spits them out." "They wanted me to make an informed decision because they did not want to risk losing a high-profile female role model in the company," she explains. Adriane admits that at first she was nervous, but weighing the risks, she reasoned that the odds weighed in her favor: the company was focused on diversity, so she would enjoy visibility; some familiar mentors were still available to her; and she had a solid track record. She decided to accept a new role in the division on the staff of the division general manager (DGM).

"Those ladies were right," recalls Adriane, now president and CEO of Honeywell Transportation Systems. There was a clear "inner circle" of four or five white males whose opinions the GM respected. And she quickly learned that three or four of them were not excited about her joining the team. It didn't take Adriane long to figure out her strategy for solidifying her position and winning their support. She focused on three main areas:

Generating buy-in. "Going in, I decided to make them a part of the business strategy I was charged to develop. In other words, try to get buy-in to avoid backlash." She set up one-on-ones with each of her peers, asked about their background, and shared hers. She reviewed the objectives she had been given and explained the operating model, but also asked for their insights about how to achieve those goals within the culture of the division. "I rolled all the input along with my own insights and presented the conclusions at a staff meeting. I got buy-in."

Observing and assessing the situation. Brown's first six months was not a cakewalk. Even after generating buy-in from her new colleagues on overall objectives, she noticed that she was not invited to key meetings, not included in decision-making, and regularly excluded from inner-circle discussions. They had a diminished view of her role, she says.

Enlisting the support of her supervisor—a respected member of the team. The attitude of her coworkers was distressing, but Adriane focused on how to work within the system to change their behavior. In a one-on-one meeting with her GM, she expressed her concerns. They agreed on three solutions: "First, that he would not go to my peers and tell them to play nice with me because they really didn't get it and wouldn't know what to do differently. Next, I told him I would no longer invite myself to meetings where I should have been included—and asked that he stop any meeting in which I should be a participant and ask for me. And finally, I shared my observations on his inner circle, and asked if he thought I could grow in my career to become a player on his team through his own inclusive behavior." The third part of that agreement made him accountable for her success. "Two years later, he selected me to run his largest business, and I eventually succeeded him as the DGM."

COACHING TIPS

That and other experiences, says Adriane, taught her several very important lessons:

Be flexible. Culture and environment are important, but there's more than one way to approach your job, she says: "Even when you think you don't need help, be open to different approaches."

Don't be a complainer. That way, when you do complain, it is heard, advises Adriane. "Be willing to offer solutions that can be acted upon."

Make sure you deliver results. "You have to be relevant for folks to take a stand to help you be successful. Deliver your commitments."

Always maintain your professionalism. You will always encounter "jerks," she says. Don't ever let them get the best of you.

ADDITIONAL COACHING TIPS FOR WOMEN

Play the politics. Women often believe that playing politics implies playing underhandedly. Most would prefer to stay independent of the "games" and "just do their work." If you want to reach the highest ranks of an organization, however, being engaged means understanding not only the political structure of your organization, but how to effectively navigate it. You can't score points if you're sitting on the bench. Although politics can be dirty, it is possible to play strategically with integrity.

Stay connected to the industry and to your network. It's important not just to join industry organizations, but also to become active in them. Run for an office, join a committee, and develop a program. Accept invitations to speak at events and moderate panels in areas of your expertise. It is through your involvement in industry programs and events that you will not only build important relationships but raise your professional profile as well. People not only see you, they can see your expertise, the quality of your work, and your knowledge of the industry. This will also force you to keep current on business trends and concerns. Alonzo says that because of her active involvement in industry organizations, her profile in the industry helped her negotiate a strong package as she exited her company, and has led to her joining the management team as an owner in her current business undertaking.

It is also important to maintain a high level of engagement even if you decide to leave the workforce for a specific period of time. When Debra Sandler left her position as vice president of marketing for PepsiCo Inc.'s Tricon Restaurants in 1997 to have a baby, she decided to stay out for no longer than two and a half years. After eighteen months, she decided to begin her search for reentry into the market and found tremendous resistance. The employers' response to Sandler was consistent with the study *Back in the Game: Returning to Business After a Hiatus* by Monica McGrath, Marla Driscoll, and Mary Gross (Wharton Center for Leadership and Change Management, June 2005). It found that women who voluntarily "step out" or "off-ramp" for a number of reasons, including raising a family or caring for a sick parent, were perceived as less competent for having left the industry. Sandler stayed in touch with contacts in her network throughout the time she was on leave. Authors of the study also recommend staying in touch with managers, attending conferences, and even seeking training and education while out of work. Sandler found an offer that satisfied her at Johnson & Johnson five months after she began her search. She joined as vice president of worldwide marketing for the J&J unit McNeil Specialty Products Co. in May 1999. Today she is worldwide president for McNeil Nutritionals LLC, overseeing the launch and marketing of Splenda, the number one artificial sweetener in America.

9

Stay Current to Remain Relevant

Being a Continuous Learner Is a Must

So, you think you've finally arrived. You have your college degree, the director or VP title, the nice office, and the big salary. Perhaps you even have seniority and have developed good relationships at the senior level. Life is good, and your career is sailing smoothly along. To keep it sailing, all you have to do is keep performing well in your current role, and all will be well, right? The fact of the matter is, nothing could be further from the truth. Not only will it take more to continue to progress in your career, it will also take more just to maintain where you are!

The demands of today's global economy have ramped up expectations. Companies are competing on so many levels, with far more regulatory policies in place. Organizations are conforming to more political, social, and ethical pressures, and technology is driving the pace of how business is conducted. If you expect to be a "continuous player" in the corporate game, you must be committed to being a "continuous learner" as well!

"Business leaders have to be continuous learners because they have to reinvent themselves several times over the course of a career," explains Michael J. Critelli, executive chairman of Pitney Bowes. "External conditions have radically changed during my career, particularly in the last ten to fifteen years." He says there are several particular factors that have keenly impacted how companies manage their businesses:

- **The Internet.** "[It] has created business models that were not possible before, [and] has given all of us, particularly as customers, so much more information and power, and has enabled real-time communications that has accelerated the pace of business."

- **Political and social volatility.** "9/11, pandemics, global warming, and much more political instability have significantly increased the importance of enterprise risk management."

- **Stiffer regulations.** "Investors, the SEC, governance rating services like ISS, and public accounting firms have put much more pressure on public companies to deliver stronger results, to be more transparent, to have better governance, and to drive share price increases."

- **Competition.** "[It's] getting tougher and more global, and business generally is sourcing employees, partners and vendors, and technology from a global marketplace."

- **Corporate social responsibility.** Companies can no longer just be concerned about profits. They are now accountable for how they treat domestic and foreign workers, how they handle the environment, and how they embrace diversity. "It has become far more important as a factor in how businesses function."

The pressure of keeping up with such demands can seem overwhelming. With an already airtight work schedule, how does a busy executive expect to stay not only current but ahead of the trends? "Executives have to stay focused and to screen out materials that are not of high value," Critelli urges. "One of the skills executives need to develop is to manage their time and their priorities to know what, among the many messages coming at them, should get their attention. In fact, Andy Grove, one of the greatest corporate leaders of the last fifty years, has said that the art of leadership is to select from among many important tasks and actions the two or three critical, highest-leverage actions that should be taken. Executives also need to be able to separate what is important, as opposed to what is urgent but less important, and to delegate tasks to others that they are capable of doing."

Although being a continuous learner is important for everyone working in the corporate world, this reality is imperative for minority managers because, again, minorities have to deal with perception issues and very often find themselves in an environment where they have to prove themselves daily.

✦ Melvin's Big Mistake

Melvin's story is an all-too-familiar example of how many minorities fail to stay current and neglect continuous learning, and how it can hinder career growth. Melvin began his corporate career after a brief stint in the military. His plan was to enlist in the military, then take advantage of military benefits and earn his college degree. After the military, however, Melvin married and, with a child on the way, decided to enter the work world. He began his career as a customer service representative for his local phone company; thanks to his gift of gab and persuasive personality, however, his sales results caught the attention of his supervisor, who recommended him for a higher-paying position as an outside sales representative in the company's sales department. Melvin nailed the interview, won the job, and was headed to sales training. Though Melvin had planned to pursue his college degree, taking advantage of his company's tuition reimbursement program, he postponed doing so and instead decided he could always do so later. After several successful years, Melvin was promoted into sales management and was now earning a six-figure salary in the company's cellular division. At this point, he determined that he had no use for a college degree and abandoned his plans to pursue one. It was around this time that his company was acquired by a competitor who operated in the same market. Melvin was informed that since they only needed one sales director for that particular market, he would have to interview for the position along with another candidate who worked in the same geography.

Melvin was certain that his track record of success and his ten years of service would be the deciding factor and win him the job. Needless to say, he was shocked to learn that in fact the other candidate, who had less experience, and whose sales results were good, but not as good as Melvin's, got the position! Instead of getting the job, Melvin got offered his choice of a demotion from director to manager or a basic severance package consisting of two weeks' pay for every year with the company, which amounted to less than six months in pay. Infuriated, Melvin demanded an audience with the hiring manager to understand why, with his better track record, he had not won the job. What he learned in that conversation was life-changing! The hiring manager shared with Melvin this message: "If we were only interviewing for a sales director to perform the existing role, you most likely would have been our selection. But in fact we were looking for an individual not only to lead our sales effort but who could eventually take over the general manager's role in two or three years. Not only do you not have a college degree, but there was nothing in your background to suggest you understood anything other than the sales function, and during the interview you demonstrated little to no knowledge of what it takes to run or manage the other functions."

While Melvin may never know for sure if he could have been successful in the general manager role, one thing was certain. His decision to postpone his education and his contentment to rest on his past success cost him the opportunity to find out.

WHY IS IT SO IMPORTANT TO BE A CONTINUOUS LEARNER?

While I could offer more than a dozen reasons that this subject is so important, I will focus on a few critical reasons:

Corporations are more focused on talent than ever before. In today's competitive business climate, companies are looking to differentiate themselves in the marketplace. One area they have increasingly focused on in recent years is the quality and caliber of talent they have in their organization. In fact, when most companies discuss their assets, many will quickly acknowledge that their "human capital"—that is, the people they employ—is what gives them an edge in the marketplace. The net result is that companies today are waging an increasingly intense battle for talent. While in the past most companies looked to gain a competitive advantage by upgrading the processes and technology infrastructure they had in place, they have now come to realize that it takes people, process, and technology to be a winner in today's global economy, with a new emphasis on people.

This can actually work to the benefit of minority managers. For decades now, the media and census data have suggested that in the United States, for example, minorities will soon become the majority of new entrants to the workforce. With that in mind, most companies set about creating diversity organizations within their human resource organizations to begin to identify and recruit diverse talent. Over the past several years there has been a noticeable increase in companies with dedicated recruiting efforts focused on minority talent. Organizations such as the National Black MBA Association (NBMBAA), the National Society of Hispanic MBAs (NSHMBA), the National Sales Network (NSN), and the National Urban League (NUL) have all witnessed increased attendance at their annual career fairs by Fortune 1000 companies and others who not only are renting booths at the fairs but coming with open job requisitions that they intend to fill with minority talent. Each year hundreds of young minorities come to these events with a résumé, and leave with a job!

Recent statistics support this trend of an ever-increasing minority population. The 2005 U.S. Census Report stated that four states are now "majority-minority"* states: Hawaii (which has long been such a state, and is the only state that has never had a white majority) and more recently New Mexico, California, and Texas. Additionally, in August 2006 the U.S. Census reported that the percentage of non-Hispanic white residents had fallen below 60 percent in Mary-

---

Majority-minority state is a term used to describe a U.S. state in which a majority of the state's population differs from the majority population of non-Hispanic whites.

land, Georgia, and Nevada. To further emphasize this trend, an August 2007 Associated Press article reported that whites are now the minority in nearly one in ten U.S. counties.

This is exciting news, as minorities are now poised to make greater gains in the corporate world as corporations come to terms with the business need to hire diverse talent. The challenge for minorities is not only to be prepared for today's job market, but to stay current to remain relevant as the market and industry dynamics change.

The playing field is more crowded, and the players more competitive. It doesn't take a rocket scientist to realize that today's workforce is quite different from that of years gone by. For starters, we have moved from an economy based primarily on manufacturing to a service industry environment. The industrial age in which companies like the Big Three automakers (Ford, Chrysler, and GM), tire and rubber companies, and the big steel companies dominated the landscape is a thing of the past. In fact, many cities that built their economies on these industries and have failed to reinvent themselves are struggling mightily. Detroit has seen its economy virtually evaporate with the demise of the Big Three, and Cleveland, once home to major steel companies, was named the Poorest Big City in the United States by the 2004 U.S. Census, with a 31.3 percent poverty rate. As a result, there are fewer jobs in the manufacturing space, and workers in those companies can be at a disadvantage when forced to compete for jobs with those from service industry backgrounds.

Second, with outsourcing and offshoring of jobs to countries such as India, the Philippines, and other Third World nations, many who work in specialized areas such as software programming, call center operation, and help desk support may soon wake up to find that they have been displaced by a worker three thousand miles away who will work for 60 percent less. While the words *outsourcing* and *offshoring* may have been taboo in the 1980s and '90s, today I would argue that most of the Fortune 100 companies in America have either begun to offshore work overseas or are planning to.

✦ Ruth's Story:
How Outsourcing and Offshoring Impacted Her Twice

Ruth began her career right out of college working in the retail banking division of a major U.S. bank. She started, like many, in a retail banking development program working in various departments, from being a teller to processing checks, while learning the retail banking business. After finishing the program, she settled into her role as a manager of the bank's call center, handling credit card customer care. Over the years she progressed in her career. While her bank was ultimately purchased by another banking institution, Ruth was able to survive and was even given greater responsibility. One day she received a call from her boss, asking her to meet with a consultant the bank had hired to help increase productivity in the call center. Being a team player, Ruth embraced the consultant and spent the better part of a week showing the consultant every aspect of the call center operations. Shortly thereafter, an announcement was made that in an effort to focus on the bank's "core competencies," the bank's call center operations would be outsourced to a company that specialized in call center operations!

Though Ruth was heartbroken, she was pleased to learn that both she and her staff would retain their jobs and salaries, but would now be employed by the outside company instead of the bank. Undaunted, Ruth took it all in stride and went to work for her new employer, determined to prove herself all over again. Unfortunately, she never really got the chance, and the other shoe dropped. Less than eighteen months after her job was outsourced to another company, this new company decided to offshore this particular call center's workload to a company based in India. The transition was completed within six months, and Ruth and her entire staff were out of work. While she eventually landed a job with another bank, to this day Ruth is always concerned that any day she could get another phone call, telling her that her job has been sent offshore.

• • •

The third contribution to the overcrowded playing field is that there are more MBAs in the marketplace and in MBA programs today than ever before. In the United States an estimated 80,000–90,000 students graduate each year with an MBA degree. With the growth of online universities, this number can only continue to increase over the next decade. The net result is, you will have more new entrants in the job market each year, trying to move up the same ladder you are on. If you are not dedicated to continuous learning, it is only a matter of time before these new MBAs will be climbing past you!

Well-read, up-to-date managers are more impressive. One of the secrets that many minorities are still not aware of is that whenever you are in the presence of a senior leader of your company, you are in fact being interviewed. It may not be a formal interview, and there may not be a job available at the time, but nevertheless, you are being interviewed. Your body language, your appearance, and, most important, your conversation are all being studied and filed away in the senior leader's mental Rolodex. Why is your conversation so important to the senior leader? Because she is always on the lookout for talent capable of adding more value in the organization. Good leaders understand that the future of their organization lies in its ability to identify, attract, and retain top talent. Your body language gives a limited indication of who you are; your appearance speaks to your professional image; but your conversation speaks volumes as to your intellect and thought process.

While a senior leader may be interested briefly in the score of the latest basketball game, or who made it to the next round of *American Idol*, she is more interested in how much you know about the company, how current you are on the latest trends in the industry, and your thoughts on the latest business book on the *New York Times* Best Sellers List. While you are speaking, she is asking herself:

- How well does this person understand the company's mission?
- How clear is this manager on the goals of the organization?
- How well does he understand the company's value proposition?
- How would this person handle himself at a client meeting, board meeting, etc.?
- Could this person carry on a conversation with other senior leaders?

None of these questions can be answered if your conversation is never elevated above the latest episode of *Lost*.

✦ A Missed Opportunity to Impress the CEO

At Pitney Bowes, CEO Murray Martin has made it his mission to make the company more effective by taking advantage of the synergies of various business units to build one company for growth. His personal challenge for all his employees is "Think As One, Act As One, Operate As One, to deliver what no other company can." He says it on every message to the field, in the company's annual report, and every time he engages with an employee on a personal level. Ironically, at one of his quarterly update meetings I had the opportunity to sit next to a young manager who was eager to ask the CEO a question. After raising his hand to get the microphone, he asked his long-awaited question. As he prepared to answer the young man's question, Martin stated, "I'll answer your question if you can tell me, what is our company goal?" The young man stood in a room crowded with midlevel and senior-level leaders, looking like a deer caught in headlights. He attempted to mumble a few words, when several of us whispered to him, "Think As One, Act As One, Operate As One." Extremely embarrassed, the young manager sat down, realizing he had just missed an opportunity.

✦ *Making the Most of an Opportunity*

At a recent World Business Forum sponsored by HSM Americas in New York City, many of the world's top business leaders addressed an audience of more than 2,500 executives over a two-day period. Speakers such as Bill Clinton, Jack Welch, Rudy Giuliani, and others spoke on topics that impact business from the local to the global stage. As part of the event, several of the speakers held private luncheons for major corporations and their key guests. At one such luncheon, the speaker was Renée Mauborgne, one of the cowriters of the international best-selling book *Blue Ocean Strategy*. Randall, a minority manager who worked at a large technology company, was at the luncheon with both his client and the CEO of his company.

As fate would have it, after her brief talk, Mauborgne took a seat at the same table as Randall and his client and CEO. As the conversation started about her book, guests at the table took turns giving their thoughts on the book and how they could apply its principles within their business. A few guests, embarrassed because they had not read the book, looked at Randall to see if he had anything meaningful to add to the discussion. Not only had Randall read the book prior to coming to the event, he was able to relate how the Cirque du Soleil example mentioned in it actually caused him to re-think the customer experience within his organization. It was a home run! Not only was the author flattered, but Randall's credibility went up with his client, and his CEO was duly impressed. Had he not been a continuous learner and paid attention to best-selling business authors, he would have looked as uninformed and unimpressive as the others at the table who had no idea what a blue ocean strategy was. Do you think this made an impression on his client and CEO? Will his CEO remember this incident the next time he hears Randall's name at a meeting or sees him in the hallway? You bet it will!

COACHING TIPS

In today's corporate world, it can be nearly impossible to stay current on every possible subject or buy and read every business book, magazine, and newspaper. Between the demands of the job, reading and writing e-mails, responding to voice mails from your office phone and cell phone, and your BlackBerry addiction, you may find it difficult to even consider going back to school or joining a professional organization. However, you need to make being a continuous learner a way of life. Below are a few suggestions on how to stay current, and remain relevant:

Read as much as you can. Stay current with the latest business books, and don't let the sheer volume of books overwhelm you; there are ways to keep up without reading every book word for word. For example, I subscribe to *Executive Book Summaries*, which gives me the gist and overview of many new books. Or you can just read a few pages of a book in bookstores: skim quickly, so you're at least familiar with some of the content; if someone at work mentions this book at a meeting, you can at least join in the conversation. Another great way to browse is at airport bookstores, because they typically have the best sellers, so you'll know what the leading books of the day are. Often, all you need to know is the title of the latest books; nobody expects you to read everything that's published.

Become active in an industry organization. "Industry-related and professional organizations can supplement what senior leaders learn from their own life and business experience," offers Michael Critelli. "They should make sure, however, that they are continually looking at their situation from an outside-in perspective, which is best given by leading-edge customers and experts from outside their industry and their typical market spaces."

Subscribe to your industry-specific publications. You *must* keep up with what's happening in your industry, but again, this doesn't mean you have to read every magazine and journal cover to cover. However, you should at least read the cover of each new issue, to see what topics are being addressed, and flip through the magazine: you'll be amazed at how much you can pick up by just skimming.

Then if you find an article that's really pertinent to your job or your company, you can read that article in its entirety. But headlines alone will tell you a lot.

Learn new skills. Remember COBOL and Fortran? Many readers probably won't, because these were the computer programs of the early 1980s. Today's programmers don't need to know these computer languages; instead, they need to know HTML so they can design Web pages—and that's exactly what André did. He was an IBM programmer who realized that mainframe programming was passé: he took a course on how to create Web sites, and André has an entirely new career now. He reinvented himself before he became obsolete—and he's wealthier than he ever expected to be because he got in early in the Internet Web site development craze.

Learn a new language. For example, if you're working in an industry that operates in a global economy, you may need to learn Japanese, Spanish, or even Chinese, because China is finally opening up to world trade. Or you may find that some other language is more important to your particular industry.

Know that there are many ways to learn. "[There] is self-learning, training, coaching and mentoring, and developmental assignments," explains Critelli. "All of those ways should be used. The individual should not be afraid to take on a less glamorous developmental assignment, particularly if there is great learning opportunity and the organization needs someone to do the assignment. I took responsibility for human resources in 1990. Many outside mentors told me that HR was not a career-enhancing position, but I did it because Pitney Bowes needed me to do the job, and it was a great developmental opportunity. My predecessor George Harvey told me that he took a special assignment in fixing a collections problem in the early 1970s and that his career was enhanced as well."

• • •

The bottom line is to find out what *you* need to know to stay current in *your* job, *your* company, and *your* industry—and then make sure that you do. Doing so will not only make you more successful in your current job; it may be your stepping stone to your next job!

10

Mentors and Sponsors

Why You Need Them
and How to Attract Them

I have described and explained throughout this book how difficult it can be to navigate the corporate landscape. And as easy as it is to see that racism and sexism (both subliminally and blatantly) obviously play a part in the difficulties and challenges that face minorities, there are so many more intricate factors that can influence your success or demise in the workplace. I have a friend who used to half-jokingly review personal challenges at work by asking herself, "Is it because I'm black?" When she confessed, among a group of friends, that this was the question she would pose when she couldn't determine the root of a problem, we all laughed—albeit uneasily. We all understood exactly what she meant. Many times it can be hard to tell. Was it my minority status that caused me to be overlooked for a promotion, or was it because I didn't develop the right cross-organizational skills for the position? It can be quite frustrating trying to decipher corporate responses. Was it race that denied me this opportunity, or were there misperceptions surrounding my abilities as a leader?

If in my mind, I've done everything that seems necessary to be viewed as the best candidate for the position/opportunity/reward, I have to ask whether racism played a role.

The answer could be yes, no, or a combination of both. It's not unusual for a manager's decision to promote another candidate, particularly a white candidate, to be influenced heavily by certain prejudices. At a convention gathering of minority professionals who sit on corporate boards, a white senior executive confessed that he worked with a number of other executives who held racist views and that prejudices influenced how they interacted with persons of color at work.

Less overt cultural biases, held by the minority candidates as well as by their managers, can also influence behavior. For example, studies have shown that white managers are often reluctant to offer constructive criticism to minority employees for fear that it will be seen as a racial attack. As a result, minority employees miss the opportunity to get the feedback necessary for their growth and development in the organization. It has also been observed that minorities at work are less likely to share personal information with coworkers or spend extended social time with them. Consequently, minorities are less likely to develop the types of networking relationships that are key to developing a professional profile within the company.

An executive coach shared a story of a young man from South America whose managers complained that there was an issue with his dress presentation. When asked about his attire, the employee reported that he didn't quite understand what the problem was. Apparently, the young man liked to roll up his sleeves when he worked, as was the custom in his native country. He didn't realize that it was inappropriate for business in the United States. But his managers also didn't feel comfortable enough to address the issue. In their mind, he was simply unprofessionally dressed. In his mind, he hadn't the slightest hint that it was a problem.

The frustration for minority professionals is not knowing the real reasons for certain consequences—not being able to properly assess or decode the information that you are receiving so that you can make the necessary changes to improve your status within your company. Pair those challenges with a company's unique culture and the business expectations of an increasingly competitive work environment, and you then easily realize why you need more than just the right degrees and a strong work ethic to make it to a corner office in corporate America. You need a network, of which the most important members are your mentors and sponsors. I like to call them your decoders and quarterbacks.

WHO ARE MENTORS AND SPONSORS?
WHY ARE THEY IMPORTANT?

For the minority professional, mentors and sponsors will serve a variety of roles and functions throughout your career, particularly if your goal is to reach the senior levels of an organization. Mentors in the initial stage will help you build that foundation and set the pace for your career. Mentoring increases again in importance as you begin to make transitions through various levels of management: from first-line management to middle management and then again from middle management to senior management.

Because these relationships evolve over the years, some will be temporary; some will last a lifetime. Some mentors and sponsors will become your friends, while others maintain a gurulike status.

In any case, they will be your most important advisors and your strongest advocates in a corporation.

But according to David A. Thomas, a Harvard professor in the Graduate School of Business Administration, in a three-year study entitled *The Truth About Mentoring Minorities: Race Matters*, for minority professionals to be successful, their mentors must be fully engaged in a variety of developmental roles, "such as that of coach, advocate, and counselor and understand the importance of each at different stages of their protégé's career . . . and also be aware of the challenges race can present to [their] protégé's career development and advancement." Thomas offers an example of a black employee managed by a white manager who was told that he needed to be more aggressive in the workplace; after he followed his mentor's advice, however, he was labeled "an angry black man." While the white manager meant well, his employee might have benefited more by having a minority mentor to discuss this with as well. It is possible that a minority mentor could have offered a different perspective on *how* to be more assertive as a minority professional without coming across as angry.

In his study, Thomas found that "promising" white professionals entered the fast track early in their career. "High-potential" minority professionals, however, typically don't take off until they reach middle management. And even at that stage the trajectory for minorities as opposed to whites is very different. In a nonsupportive environment or without the help of engaged mentors, minority professionals can become disheartened and frustrated. Thomas explains that mentors of successful professionals not only offer career advice and guidance but are instrumental in keeping promising minorities on track, building confidence as well as competence, and helping them establish credibility within their company.

But how do you develop and nurture these relationships? There is a process, a work ethic, and an etiquette, all of which you must properly manage. Although mentors and sponsors will play similar roles in helping to advance your career, there are significant differences between the two.

MENTORS—DECODERS OF INFORMATION

According to Sheila Wellington, former Catalyst president and author of *Be Your Own Mentor: Strategies from Top Women on the Secrets of Success*, mentors are the single most important factor in success in the workplace. Why? Mentors are the persons inside and outside of an organization who best know the terrain. Mentors outside the company know the industry. Their expertise is rooted in a history of industry changes and evolutions; they also have a good sense of what future trends and challenges are in store. They also know the players in the industry. If they don't know them personally, they understand how they do business.

Inside an organization, mentors understand the culture of the company—its formal and informal structures. In other words, they know the business expectations for the company, its growth and priority areas. But they also understand the company's management style, the idiosyncrasies of the management team—strengths, weaknesses, and vulnerabilities—and what management looks for in a person they consider a team player or a leader. If you don't have a clear understanding of your company's expectations, those outlined as well as the unwritten rules, you become a long shot in trying to win desired promotions.

Mentor relationships can be formal or informal. An increasing number of organizations are recognizing the benefit of such unions and offer formal mentoring programs. It was through the African

American Forum (AAF), General Electric's affinity organization, that Alfreda met Paula Madison, executive vice president of diversity at NBC Universal.* Their program suggests that mentors change mentees every two years, but Alfreda has enjoyed the benefits of Paula's more than seventeen years of network experience since 2003. It was Paula who recommended that Alfreda introduce the company's chairman at an annual AAF symposium. Her performance was a success, and it created a spotlight opportunity for the general counsel in increasing her visibility and expanding her network.

Informal mentoring relationships can be just as fulfilling and rewarding. In the absence of a formal program, however, it is up to the individual—the mentee—to select an appropriate mentor and help manage the relationship. Informal mentoring also allows the opportunity to have several mentors. In fact, most senior-level executives will admit that a variety of key professionals internally and externally have advised them on their careers.

✦ Ron's Story:
How a Mentor Helped Connect the Dots

Often a mentee can be so close to his own personal situation that he can't see the forest for the trees. Perhaps he has always had his heart set on a certain job or position. Maybe he chose a certain discipline such as finance or sales, and, for whatever reason, can't envision doing anything else. It is during times like this that a good mentor can prove invaluable. Ron was a successful minority sales manager who worked in Detroit for a company that sold aftermarket accessories

---

*Wendy Harris, "Making the Connection," *Black Enterprise*, February 2007.

for the automobile industry. Growing up in Detroit, Ron wanted to live in Detroit and work for Ford, Chrysler, or General Motors. Over the years he had developed a mentoring relationship with an executive from IBM. This mentor began to challenge Ron on how his skills, though almost exclusively in the automobile industry, could be transferable to a company like IBM. His mentor was concerned that, given the woes of the American automobile manufacturers, Ron could be inadvertently hindering his career growth.

Ron's mentor was able to show him how he could leverage his experience in calling on the automotive industry, and how that would position him for advancement in another company whose future was not linked to any particular industry. Though it was hard for his ego, Ron accepted a position as a senior account manager at a major telecommunications company, calling on Chrysler. Because of his extensive knowledge of the automobile industry and its challenges, Ron was able to leverage that knowledge and became a top performer in no time. After two years in a sales role, he was promoted to manager, and later director. When his company was acquired by SBC, he was promoted to a strategic position in Atlanta. Recently, Ron and I had the chance to reconnect, and he admitted that had he not listened to the advice of his mentor and reinvented himself, he might still be in Detroit, unemployed, with a home he might not be able to sell given the economic condition of the city and the industry.

✦ *Connie's Story:*
How a New Hire Benefited from a Mentor

Because mentors will have more intimate knowledge of business directives, they can often give solid advice on how best to steer your career, even if you have other expectations for your growth. When Connie joined the Northern Trust Company in the marketing department, her mentor suggested she transition to sales to manage one of their teams, although she had no sales experience. Recognizing her strengths and talents as a leader, and seeing that she demonstrated a clear understanding of their clients and their products, he believed that her skills were transferable. "He made it very clear that we are a sales culture, and one of the most important ways to learn the business and to advance is to take this opportunity in sales," she explained in an article in *Black Enterprise* magazine. She followed his advice and eventually became senior vice president and deputy business unit head in charge of financial management, strategic planning, business continuity, and disaster recovery. While it is always a good idea to have a mentor, it can be even more valuable when you have joined a new organization. In a new company, the mentor can help you understand the culture, the key players, and even those to avoid. As stated previously, every company has its own unique culture, and it pays to have a mentor to serve as a guide.

SPONSORS—YOUR QUARTERBACKS
TO THE END GOAL

I had a friend whose television production company was experiencing budget constraints, which she knew would result in layoffs. She was stunned, however, to learn how management decided who would stay and who would go. They literally put names in a box, and as each name was called, unless an executive spoke on that person's behalf, vouching for her performance and financial worth to the company, that person was eliminated. People without sponsors were let go.

On a corporate level, the process for deciding a player's worth is not often this simplistic or linear, but in this example the role of a sponsor is very clear. Sponsors are inner-circle players, high-level executives who drive and influence decisions made on your behalf. They also can speak and negotiate on your behalf in quarters and boardroom discussions that you are not a part of, or sometimes even aware of. Sponsors, like mentors, will also offer you directional advice and make recommendations on your intended career path. There is one significant difference between the two, however. Mentors, you choose. Sponsors choose you.

✦ Ellis's Story:
How a Sponsor Can Make a Real Difference

Ellis was a young, charismatic African American director of sales for a leading communications company. He had built a successful track record over his ten-year career with the company, and was ready for the next level. However, because he was in his early thirties, many in the company felt he was not yet mature enough from a business perspective to become a vice president. Previous leadership valued Ellis, but at the same time felt that his age and youthful appearance would not allow him to be taken seriously by employees, clients, or senior leaders in the company. As Ellis began to become more disenchanted, he noticed that a certain senior VP had begun to reach out to him. This senior VP, who also happened to be an African American, was new to the company, and as part of learning more about the challenges of the business, he invited Ellis to lunch. After observing Ellis over the next six months, the senior VP decided to become a sponsor for Ellis. Roughly a month after that meeting, Ellis received a call from headquarters, asking him to participate in a corporate initiative to improve client satisfaction. As a part of this project he had the opportunity to meet with key leaders in the organization, including the chief operating officer. Soon after, Ellis received a call from Human Resources asking if he would be interested in a division VP role in Chicago. This call came during the company's annual succession planning session, at which his sponsor campaigned for Ellis to be placed on the interview slate. Because of personal reasons, Ellis was not able to relocate at this time, but now his sponsor had positioned him for success. A second VP role became available six months later in Kansas City, and while he was not the leading candidate, Ellis did interview for the role and gained additional exposure.

During this time, Ellis continued to meet periodically with his sponsor, and together they created a development plan that included Ellis taking executive-level training from an Ivy League continuing-education program. Finally, a VP position became available that would not require relocation, and Ellis was selected, becoming one of the youngest VPs in the company's history.

GETTING MENTORS AND SPONSORS TO SIGN ON

As I mentioned earlier, mentors are professionals you choose, and sponsors are executives who choose you. I look for people who have both the assertiveness and the preparedness to seek me out, a clear understanding of what it is they're trying to achieve, and an awareness of their own strengths as well as lesser strengths. But above all, I look for those who are willing to put in the work to grow and develop.

When I sponsor, I'm putting my name and my credibility on the line. So when I look for minority professionals to sponsor, I look for individuals who have demonstrated consistent high performance throughout their career and who are excelling in their current role. But there is a process to go through as well as several considerations to get mentors and sponsors to sign on as your professional advisors and advocates and to make sure that these relationships truly work to your benefit and for your intended career goals.

Be exemplary. Before you can ask someone to be your mentor, you have to be someone worth mentoring. Mentoring is all about helping to nurture talent to its fullest potential, developing promising professionals into great leaders. It becomes a source of pride for a mentor. Conversely, no one in a corporate environment has time to waste on an employee who is less than professional.

Kim Bianca Williams, performance improvement consultant and owner of VCL Consulting Group, Inc., identifies specific character qualities that mentees should possess if they desire to engage in successful mentoring relationships. First, a mentee must be teachable. Too often, mentees seek mentoring relationships to promote their own personal agenda. Mentees must understand that mentoring relationships are not for the purpose of getting a free ride on the coattails of an experienced professional. Mentoring relationships are designed to enhance performance, both personally and professionally. Therefore, the mentee must be willing to learn. And learning involves being open to constructive criticism, being willing to identify and examine areas that need improvement, and being ready to embrace new ideas and methods of accomplishing goals.

Second, a mentee must be willing to take calculated risks. There will be occasions when a mentor's guidance seems a little risky. Perhaps he will encourage the mentee to enter into unfamiliar territory. However, if a strong relationship has been developed, and it is undergirded by trust, know that the best interest of the mentee is at the forefront. The only way that people can grow and develop is by allowing themselves to stretch beyond their normal limitations.

Finally, mentees must be passionate. The old adage, "You can lead a horse to water, but you can't make him drink," still rings true as it pertains to the success of a mentoring relationship. While a mentor's responsibility is to provide the mentee with guidance and opportunities that will lead her toward her goal, it is the responsibility of the mentee to "take the walk." Good ideas come and go. Emotions change from day to day. Circumstances may cause one to wonder, Am I on the right path? But passion says, "Regardless of external forces, I am committed to the cause; doing my best and being my best, despite impeding conditions."

Identify executives with experience and influence. It is best to choose mentors senior to you in their position in the company. Ideally, these individuals are well respected in the organization and can influence decisions on some level.

Create your own "board of directors." You should plan to have more than one mentor, and different mentors as you progress and develop in your career. It is important to have mentors who look like you, but it is also vital to develop mentoring relationships with professionals of varying ethnic backgrounds, as long as you agree to be honest about the exchange of information, which may include discussions about race and gender. In David A. Thomas's study (see page 189), he recounts a situation where a white mentor was bothered by his African American mentee's "abrasive" style, but felt that if he confronted him about it, the mentee would see it as a racial attack. You and your mentor must be able to talk openly and honestly about the attitudes, opinions, and stereotypes surrounding race and gender.

Manage the relationship. As much as mentors are viewed as advisors or advocates, they are people with families, hectic schedules, and work challenges. A mentee can reap huge rewards from this relationship, but because it is a relationship, the mentee should when possible reciprocate with information, help on a project, and so on.

ORGANIZATIONAL MENTORING

While most of our mentoring discussion has focused on personal mentoring in a one-on-one environment, many minority organizations offer mentoring programs that involve team mentoring. Three such organizations are the National Black MBA Association, the National Society of Hispanic MBAs, and the Executive Leadership Council.

The National Black MBA Association (NBMBAA)

Considered the largest and most influential professional minority organization, the NBMBAA offers many programs to help develop its membership, even one focused on developing high-school-age youths. Their annual Leadership Institute Workshop and their Leaders of Tomorrow are two examples of how organizations can take mentoring to a whole new level.

The Leadership Institute. One day prior to the NBMBAA Annual Conference and designed for high achievers and paradigm shifters, the NBMBAA Leadership Institute annually presents a full day's worth of challenging and intensive learning encounters. Content, accountability, and results are the hallmark of the Leadership Institute. Successful participation in this day-long submersion in professional and personal development requires commitment, planning, dedication, and preparation; the results are insights and advanced strategies that can be implemented immediately and keep participants way ahead of the curve. Previous speakers have included John C. Maxwell, Jack Canfield, and Dr. Dennis Kimbro. This event typically draws over a thousand participants each year, and is used by many Fortune 1000 companies as a way to provide more specialized mentoring to their minority professionals.

Leaders of Tomorrow: Taking the average to above-average heights. One of the more unique mentoring programs offered by organizations today is the NBMBAA's Leaders of Tomorrow program. For more than a decade, this challenging program has had a stimulating influence on high school students with a grade point average between C- and C+. These students have exhibited leadership potential, but require additional motivating people and factors in their lives to realize their full potential. Local NBMBAA chapters are available to tutor, lead workshops, chaperone students on college tours and to the NBMBAA Annual Conference, and administer scholarship programs for college-bound students.

The National Society of Hispanic MBAs (NSHMBA)

The National Society of Hispanic MBAs was created in 1988. Widely known as the "Premier Hispanic Organization," NSHMBA serves thirty-two chapters and seven thousand members in the United States and Puerto Rico. It exists to foster Latino leadership through graduate management education and professional development. NSHMBA works to prepare Latinos for leadership positions throughout the United States, so that they can provide the cultural awareness and sensitivity vital in the management of the nation's diverse workforce.

Hispanic Executive Summit. The NSHMBA recently held its fourth annual Hispanic Executive Summit. During the three-day summit, over 150 Latino leaders from across the United States attended professional development, governance, and leadership sessions designed by the National Association of Corporate Directors and the Disney Institute. Attendees also engaged in roundtable discussions, networked with fellow professionals, and listened to dynamic presentations by noted business leaders. Participants in this event walk away not only with increased knowledge but also with the confidence that they are ready to make a difference in the boardroom.

The Executive Leadership Council (ELC)

As one of the most prestigious professional organizations of any kind, the ELC is committed to leadership development. While its membership is a virtual who's who of senior-level executive leadership, the organization understands the imperative to develop future leaders and has two unique programs that are designed to empower those who are looking to reach the top of the corporate ladder:

The Institute for Leadership Development & Research. In October 2003, the Executive Leadership Council launched the Institute for Leadership Development & Research. The institute was established through the generous financial contribution of founding sponsor BP. The contribution also established a legacy endowment.

The mission of the institute is to both identify and develop African American corporate leadership (high-potential and senior executives) and prepare them for diverse global leadership. Additionally, the institute will provide executive development for senior nonprofit leaders. Integral components of the institute are the research papers, publications, reviews, analyses, and recommendations offered.

The institute achieves its objectives with support from a world-class faculty and staff, alignment with universities, collaborative interest groups, and by developing acclaimed seminars and research. The following are among its objectives:

- Developing and hosting seminars for African Americans who are high-potential/high-performing/seasoned managers (within five levels of CEO).
- Developing and hosting leadership-enhancement seminars for senior African American corporate executives (within three levels of CEO).
- Creating leadership opportunities for senior African American nonprofit leaders.
- Identifying and publishing scholarly research, periodicals, publications, and op-ed articles on topics such as global leadership issues, diversity best practices, and alignment with national organizations.
- Gaining recognition as the world-class development and research institute for African American corporate leaders and business issues affecting global diversity.

NextGen Network: Preparing tomorrow's senior executives . . . today. NextGen Network Inc. was founded in 1999 as a youth affiliate of the Executive Leadership Council, the nation's premier leadership network of the most senior African American corporate executives in Fortune 500 companies. NextGen Network is a world-class professional organization that offers career and professional development, community service opportunities, and points of connectivity for African American business professionals.

NextGen Network's mission is to create a professional network and development opportunity for African American professionals, to serve as an extension of the Executive Leadership Council and its charitable affiliate, the Executive Leadership Foundation, to provide career and professional development for future business leaders, and to offer community outreach programming and support. Many members of the NextGen Network have gone on to become members of the prestigious ELC.

COACHING TIPS

Having a mentor is no replacement for performance and results. One of the misperceptions that I notice among many mentees who are new to mentoring is that now that they have a mentor, they have an inside track to a promotion or success. Nothing could be further from the truth. At the end of the day, it is still your responsibility to continue to perform and deliver results. Your mentor is not a fairy godparent who will open doors for you if you have not sustained your level of performance and are not deserving. In fact, for a mentor to do so would put you at a disadvantage, and possibly set you up for failure.

You need to come prepared when working with a mentor. Mentors are very busy people who have careers and obligations of their own. Also, they do not have the time or ability to help you in every area of your life. I strongly suggest that when you meet with your mentor for the first time, you come prepared with an idea of two to three areas in which you need coaching and direction, and focus your sessions on those areas. Ideally, you will create a mentoring plan to keep you and your mentor on track, and help both of you stay focused. Additionally, at follow-up mentoring sessions you need to begin by briefing your mentor on those activities you have accomplished since your last session.

If possible, have a set schedule to meet with your mentor. While it may not always be possible, it is a good idea to schedule your formal mentoring sessions in advance. Schedules can be hectic for both parties, and you can soon find yourself frustrated when it becomes a challenge finding time on your mentor's calendar. Try to limit each session to no more than an hour, and always conclude the session by confirming when your next discussion will take place. Likewise, do *not* make a habit of calling your mentor to discuss every question you have or every challenge you face whenever you see fit. Ideally, save these for your next session unless they are of a critical nature. Your mentor will appreciate your respecting her time.

Consider having multiple mentors. It is very important to remember that it is unlikely that any one mentor will be able to meet all of your mentoring needs. Depending on what your areas of need are, you will probably need multiple mentors. This will also mean that some of your mentors will be nonminorities. In fact, most of my own mentors have not been African American. Additionally, more than likely most of your mentoring relationships will last for a finite period. As you progress and grow in your career, you will have to periodically identify new mentors who can help you move to the next level.

Don't just have a mentor, BE a mentor! Just as it is important to seek out mentors to help guide your career, it is equally important for you to take the lessons you have learned and take time to mentor those who could benefit from your knowledge. In the next chapter we will discuss ways in which you can work with an organization that may already have formal mentoring programs in place. However, many of us only need to look at those in our family, church, or community who look up to us, and value us as role models.

11

The Importance of Giving Back

"To Whom Much Is Given,
Much Is Required"
—*Luke 12:48*

Hopefully, by now you have gained some additional insights that will help you on your professional journey. In the previous ten chapters, we have tried to share secrets to success that you can use to accelerate your growth or, at a minimum, reduce your frustration level. However, there is one more important lesson that we would like to share, and that is the importance for successful minority managers of finding ways to give back. Give back to those minorities coming up behind you, give back to your community, and give back to those organizations that have helped in your personal development, or that are focused on helping other minorities achieve. Without the help and involvement of those who are successful in our communities, our families, our people, and our collective futures will not benefit from the intellectual capital we possess, and ultimately we will never realize the potential impact we could have on the world. When we do give back, we move beyond success to significance!

SUCCESS VERSUS SIGNIFICANCE

Most of us desire on some level to be successful. While our idea of what success looks like may vary from individual to individual, no one wakes up every morning wanting to be a failure. For some, success is earning a college degree, landing a great job, and having the house with the white picket fence, a spouse, and 2.5 kids. For others, it is achieving a certain level of career success. Maybe your vision of success is a job with a vice president title and a six-figure income, or becoming a member of a prestigious country club. Recently, a colleague of mine told me that once he purchased his very own fifty-five-foot yacht, he would then consider himself a success. Whatever your definition is, there is a certain goal or goals you have identified that you believe will define you and your efforts as successful. So the question becomes: After you achieve these goals and are considered a success, then what? Sure, you could then add other goals and pursue them as aggressively as you did your previous ones, but after you've realized these new goals, the question remains the same: Then what?

Please don't misunderstand me. There is absolutely nothing wrong with having goals and pursuing success. To the contrary, I more than applaud any minority who takes the time to discipline himself, create goals for his life, and achieve them. In fact, I wish more of us were of the mind to do so. But all of the goals I listed above, as well as most things we would write down on our list of obtaining success, have one thing in common: they all die when we die! Someone else takes the VP job; the yacht, cars, and homes all eventually rust out or are destroyed; and very little is left behind. On the other hand, significance leaves a legacy. For purposes of this discussion I define *significance* as "investing your success in others in order to perpetuate it beyond your lifetime." Significance demands that you take the focus off your own pursuits, accomplishments, and possessions, and identify ways in which you can leverage your success for the good of others. Significance requires that you somehow use every award, special recognition, and honor you receive as a platform to share lessons of empowerment with others. But above all, significance requires that you leave this earth a better place than when you entered it! More enriched because you took the time to leave a lasting legacy by sharing with the world that which you had learned.

A MOMENT OF TRUTH

A few years ago I came to grips with the need for significance as I reached a high point in my life. Having just been named president at Pitney Bowes, I experienced a great sense of euphoria; I had accomplished a major life goal. Having grown up in the crime-infested inner city of Cleveland, I had no idea that life could ever take me this far. I was refused admission twice by a prestigious private grade school and forced to make the best of it in the Cleveland public school system. In high school I was labeled a troublemaker and heard my mother be told that sending me there was a waste of time and money. In college, rather than interning at a Fortune 500 company, I spent my summers flipping burgers at McDonald's and selling paint at Sears. But here I was, president of a $700 million business within a Fortune 500 company, with a salary that a few years earlier would have been unimaginable and all the trappings of success. I had a beautiful family, a McMansion of a home, and the respect and admiration of my friends and family. My garage contained a Bentley, a BMW, a convertible Lexus, and a Range Rover. I vacationed in Paris, London, and the Caribbean on a regular basis, and wore only tailor-made suits and shirts. To the world, I had it all—but something was still missing.

The reality of my situation came to me as I attended an event that was focused on the plight of the African American male in the United States. Hearing speaker after speaker shed light on the growing number of black men in the penitentiary system, coupled with the increase in the high school dropout rate, caught my attention. I later ran into a former associate who was battling depression because, even with a college degree and years of experience, he had been out of the workforce for two years. And finally, attending the funeral of a business partner who left the world without doing all he had planned, I was forced to reevaluate my life. After careful reflection, I realized that much of what I had would mean nothing after my life was over, and that unless I behaved differently, the valuable life lessons I learned would die with me. The realization hit me like a ton of bricks: success is important and a worthwhile pursuit, but it is not enough.

THE MINORITY IMPERATIVE

For most successful minorities, our quest to be the best has been a lifelong journey. Perhaps it was our parents who provided the motivation, or a special role model we observed along the way, or maybe the need to succeed came from within ourselves, but at some point something within us created a drive that has fueled our desire to be the best we can be. To be sure, none of us achieved whatever level of success we enjoy today by ourselves. All along the way there have been people, institutions, and organizations that have assisted, mentored, motivated, and even prodded us along this path. However, if we are observant and honest, we would have to agree that many of our friends, family, and colleagues haven't enjoyed the same level of support or success. While we are considered by many the "talented tenth" of our race, as Dr. W. E. B. DuBois called us, a reference that is applicable to all minority groups, the question becomes, What about the other 90 percent? Whose responsibility is it to help those who are willing but not equipped? How will those who have the drive, but not the roadmap, ever travel down the road to success without someone to show the way? Is it the responsibility of government alone to provide opportunities for those in need of direction? Should minorities be at the mercy of affirmative action or diversity programs as their only hope? Or should they, as Supreme Court justice Clarence Thomas is credited with advocating, "pull themselves up by their bootstraps"?

While I would strongly agree that both the government and big business could do more to advance the careers of talented, willing minorities, helping them to realize their full potential and live out the American dream, I would argue that those of us minorities who call ourselves successful also have a tremendous responsibility in this effort. While many of us may have tired of the African proverb "It takes a village to raise a child," the truth is, we should not leave the cause of advancing the plight of minorities to others alone. It is a minority imperative that each of us find a way to give back and help those who desire to follow in our footsteps. This effort can take many forms, from being a mentor, as discussed earlier, to something as simple as letting a young person "shadow" you for a day and observe you in the workplace. It can take the form of volunteering at your local Boys and Girls Club, or speaking at a Career Day event at your local high school. Whatever the avenue, it is the minority imperative that we take the time to help develop the next generation of leadership.

THREE EXAMPLES OF SOCIAL RESPONSIBILITY IN ACTION

Omega Psi Phi Fraternity Brothers Leading the Way

In southern California the men of Omega Psi Phi Fraternity Inc. decided over fourteen years ago that there was more they could do to help prepare young black men to develop fully into manhood. Concerned about the dropout rate of young black boys, the rise in gang activity, the lack of male role models in the community, and the overpopulation of our penitentiaries with young black men, they met to identify what they could do to reverse these trends. Their response to this challenge was the creation of the Annual Youth Leadership Conference in 1993. This event, according to Brother Ricky Lewis, who oversees the conference, attracts roughly four hundred participants each year, ages eight to eighteen, and since its inception has touched the lives of over three thousand young men. During this day-long event, the brothers of Omega meet, lecture, and role-play with these young men on the importance of social, academic, and personal responsibility. In addition, they also focus on health and wellness and the importance of maintaining one's mind, body, and soul. Programs like the Youth

Leadership Conference are so important, given the state of young black men in today's society. As the numbers below indicate, without more programs like the YLC, the outlook for young black males is not promising:

- While blacks represent less than 15 percent of the total U.S. population, the unemployment rate for African Americans is more than two times that of white Americans.*
- Nearly 25 percent of African Americans over the age of eighteen live below the poverty line, three times the percentage of whites. Of African Americans under the age of eighteen, 33.5 percent live in poverty.†
- Black men earned less than three-quarters of what white men earned in 2006, approximately $12,000 less in terms of annual median income, and only $5,000 more than black women.‡
- Among African Americans over the age of twenty-five who have less than a high school education, only 40 percent are a part of the workforce.§
- Black students make up only 17 percent of public school students, but 41 percent of special education placements, 85 percent of which are boys.**
- In the inner cities, more than half of all black men do not finish high school.††

---

* Bureau of Labor Statistics, 2006, as reported in the Special Senate Democratic report, *State of Our Union for African Americans under George W. Bush*.

† Ibid.

‡ National Urban League, *State of Black America Report*, 2007.

§ Ibid.

** *A Positive Future for Black Boys: Building the Movement* (Cambridge, MA: Schott Foundation for Public Education, 2006).

†† *New York Times*, "Plight Deepens for Black Men, Studies Warn," March 20, 2006.

- In 2000, 65 percent of black male high school dropouts in their twenties were jobless—that is, unable to find work, not seeking it, or incarcerated. By 2004 the share had grown to 72 percent, compared with 34 percent of white and 19 percent of Latino dropouts.*

- By their mid-thirties, 30 percent of black men with no more than a high school education have served time in prison.[†]

- Among black dropouts in their late twenties, more are in prison on a given day—34 percent—than are working—30 percent—according to an analysis of the 2000 census.[‡]

- Nationally, only 25 percent of black men between eighteen and twenty-four attended college in 2000. By contrast, 35 percent of black women in the same age group and 36 percent of all eighteen- to twenty-four-year-olds were attending college.[§]

- A 2006 study reported that black men were disproportionately represented in the criminal justice system—nearly three times that of Latino men and nearly seven times that of white men.[**]

- While black men represent 14 percent of the population of young men in the United States, they represent more than 40 percent of the prison population, not including young men on parole.[††]

---

* *New York Times*, "Plight Deepens for Black Men, Studies Warn," March 20, 2006.
[†] Ibid.
[‡] Ibid.
[§] American Council on Education, as reported in Bill Maxwell, "On Campus, Grim Statistics for African American Men," *St. Petersburg Times*, January 4, 2004.
[**] Kaiser Family Foundation Report, *Young African American Men in the United States*, Menlo Park, CA, July 2006.
[††] Ibid.

Thanks to the men of Omega Psi Phi, the young men that they mentor and develop are more likely to grow into manhood with a sense of purpose, and less likely to end up a statistic.

Detroit Hispanic Development Corporation: Making a Difference

Unfortunately, challenges such as those being addressed by the men of Omega are not limited to the African American community. The Latino community has also had to deal with issues ranging from gang violence and high school dropout rates to issues surrounding teen pregnancy. In an effort to combat these challenges in the southwest Detroit area, Angie Reyes founded the Detroit Hispanic Development Corporation (DHDC) in her living room in 1997. In September 2001, the agency moved to a 28,500-square-foot building to better serve the southwest Detroit community. DHDC currently has over forty dedicated staff and provides a wide range of bilingual services to over ten thousand youth, adults, and families per year.

DHDC's services include several different programs with an annual budget of over $2 million. Staff include a number of individuals who have been leaders in this community for several years in the development and implementation of youth gang, substance abuse, and violence prevention programs, alternative educational programs, parent training and advocacy, HIV/AIDS prevention education, and workforce development and counseling programs. Their programs have received national recognition for their effectiveness in helping hard-to-serve populations and reaching out to the people many others don't want—gang members, ex-offenders, families receiving public assistance, new immigrants, and individuals with substance abuse problems.

DHDC is also considered the leading organization in the regional Latino community in providing services to high-risk youth. These include several in-school, after-school, and summer programs, as well as services for those who have dropped out of school, many of them gang-involved. In September of 2005, the Detroit Hispanic Development Corporation opened the Urban Arts Academy Alternative High School. This school was born out of the need to provide alternative educational services to youth struggling to succeed in traditional classroom settings. Southwest Detroit has an 87 percent high school dropout rate; the academy is working to decrease that number using art and hip-hop culture as tools to engage students.

Again, organizations like DHDC are essential if our collective minority communities are to reach their full potential, not just for a select few, but for anyone within these communities who has the desire and will to succeed. The Latino community faces employment and other issues as well, as a study from the National Survey of America's Families indicates the following:

- Latinos are significantly more likely to be low-income (61 percent of Latinos, 49 percent of blacks, and 26 percent of whites).
- Latinos are less likely to receive child support (40 percent for Latinos, 48 percent for blacks, and 58 percent for whites).
- Latinos are most likely to report being in fair or poor health (33 percent for Latinos, 23 percent for blacks, and 20 percent for whites).
- Latinos are more likely to have uninsured children (29 percent of Latino children, 19 percent of white children, and 16 percent of black children).

- Latinos experience rates of housing hardship that are twice as high as those for whites.[*]
- There are over 283,000 Latinos in federal and state prisons and local jails, making up slightly over 15 percent of the inmate population.[†]
- Nearly one in three persons held in federal prisons is Latino.[‡]

Latino Employment Data

In July 2006, HispanicBusiness.com reported the following Latino employment data through June 2006:

- The Latino unemployment rate increased in June to 5.3 percent from 5.0 percent in May, according to data released Friday by the U.S. Department of Labor. The overall U.S. unemployment rate remained unchanged at 4.6 percent, maintaining the five-year low it reached in May.

- Latino men have one of the highest labor force participation rates of any group. In June it reached 84.9 percent, compared to the 76.0 percent participation rate of all men age twenty and over.

- The unemployment rate for Latino women twenty years and over also rose, from 5.0 in May to 5.1 percent in June. There were 55,000 new jobs for Latino women in June, not enough to absorb the increase into the labor force of 61,000 Latino women, increasing the unemployed by approximately 5,000.

- The unemployment rate for Latino youths (age sixteen to nineteen) increased by a whopping 6.3 percentage points in June, to 20.1 percent from 13.8 percent in May. With school letting out, 139,000 Latino teenagers joined the labor market. While 46,000 found work, approximately 94,000 were added to the rolls of the unemployed.[§]

---

[*] Sarah Staveteig and Alyssa Wigton, *Racial and Ethnic Disparities: Key Findings from the National Survey of America's Families* (Washington, DC: The Urban Institute, 2000).

[†] Bureau of Justice Statistics, April 2002.

[‡] Federal Bureau of Prisons population count, June 2003.

[§] Andrea Lehman, HispanicBusiness.com, July 10, 2006.

National Coalition for Asian Pacific American Community Development: Bringing Empowerment to the Asian Community

The Asian Pacific American (APA) population in the United States has been rising at a rapid rate and now represents the fastest-growing ethnic group over the past ten years. The continued increase and diversity of the APA population coupled with the recent welfare reform, HUD devolution, cutbacks in housing and education, and stricter immigration laws has made it critical for community development organizations to join together. The National Coalition for Asian Pacific American Community Development (National CAPACD) was founded in 1999 by established community development practitioners working with the Asian American Pacific Islander communities. The initiative to create a national entity grew out of an ongoing dialogue among five leading community development organizations: Asian Americans for Equality (AAFE), New York; Chinatown Community Development Center (Chinatown CDC), San Francisco; East Bay Asian Local Development Corporation (EBALDC), Oakland, California; Interim Community Development Association (ICDA), Seattle; and Little Tokyo Service Center (LTSC), Los Angeles.

The National CAPACD is a membership-based network of local community-based agencies that have been and are active players in various social and economic empowerment movements that came together after the civil rights era and developed through the War on Poverty initiatives. Over the past five years, the National CAPACD has brought together some of the most sophisticated, comprehensive, and active community development agencies, social service providers, national organizations, advocates, and organizers. Through national forums and venues to foster and make visible local indigenous leadership, it has been able to promote peer-to-peer learning through annual conventions and task forces, and link organizations and resources to broader networks. Building on the reputation of its member agencies, it has also developed strategic partnerships with national, regional, and local organizations; intermediaries; financial institutions; policy makers; and immigrant, workers' rights, and other social change movements.

THE IMPORTANCE OF GIVING BACK

An interview with Seitu Jemel Hart, director of corporate development, National Urban League, and Betty Shanahan, executive director and CEO, Society of Women Engineers:

Q: Do you believe that successful minority professionals have an obligation to give back to the community? Why?

SJH: I do not know if I like the word *obligation*, but I do think successful minority professionals should want to be resource sharers and give insight in terms of creating and sustaining a successful career. Especially since for many of us, if we are standing tall it's because our feet are on top of strong shoulders. . . .

BS: I'm focusing on the word *obligation*. I do not feel minority professionals have any more (or less) of an obligation to give back to the community than any majority professionals.

Q: Is it your opinion that most minority professionals understand this need to give back?

SJH: I would like to think when called upon to give back, many minority professionals, if time permits and it is of interest to them, will do so. However, I often find myself wondering, as minorities obtain greater financial access and more social mobility, if giving back becomes less of a priority.

BS: I do believe that more minority professionals than majority professionals recognize the support they received from others to be successful in their career and show their appreciation to their mentors and supporters by giving back to the community.

Q: How does your organization provide opportunities for senior minority professionals to give back?

SJH: My organization, through our summer internship program, the Black Executive Exchange Program (BEEP) conference, and our work within communities across the country, gives our senior minority professionals a wealth of opportunities to give back.

BS: The Society of Women Engineers and our members have numerous programs to reach girls in K–12 to make them aware of the opportunities in engineering. The organization also supports more senior professionals mentoring younger professionals and female college students.

Q: What advice would you offer minority professionals, as it pertains to the need to give back?

SJH: My advice is to do something that helps to advance someone else's life or career. If you are a minority in America, no matter how highly successful you have become, someone has helped you get there either directly or indirectly.

BS: I would encourage a minority professional to recognize the impact that we can have in a young person's life by mentoring or being a role model.

While both executives may have preferred a term less demanding than *obligation,* both recognize a need for minority professionals to give back to the community in one form or another. While we should be proud of our accomplishments in the corporate arena, and take time to celebrate our success, let us not stop at just being successful, for I firmly believe that for all minorities, success is not enough. Choose to take your success and transform it into significance. Strive to leave a lasting legacy that will help the next generation learn from our collective experiences and, in turn, achieve and accomplish even more. Then, and only then, will you move from success to significance!

12

The Importance of Not Giving Up

You May Be Closer Than You Think

As part of the introduction for this book, I included an excerpt from a book I began writing roughly fifteen years ago. The writing contained the voice of a bitter, angry, frustrated young man, who felt betrayed by everything and everyone: his early childhood experiences, which made him feel insecure about his ability to compete with his white counterparts; his educational experience, which he felt did not properly prepare him to be as competitive as his Ivy League colleagues; and especially his employers, who he felt had conspired against him and were determined to deny his potential and limit his opportunities. But now this same young man, some years later, has exceeded not only his own expectations but the expectations of those who doubted his abilities in the first place. I feel compelled to dig deeper into the journey of this young man for two simple reasons: first, because the young man in question is me, and second, to share my final message with anyone who may find themselves experiencing similar feelings, harboring similar frustrations, and finding themselves embracing the idea that life in the corporate world is not worth it. My advice in a nutshell: Don't give up!

At the time of this writing, three of the most visible minority CEOs announced their resignations. After disappointing earnings results, Stanley O'Neal agreed to resign as the chairman and CEO of Merrill Lynch, Aylwin Lewis stepped down as CEO of Sears Holdings, and Richard Parsons resigned at the end of 2007 as the CEO of AOL Time Warner, but remains as chairman. While on the surface it may appear that minorities are continuing to lose ground in the boardroom, there is also a glimmer of hope. For example, in 1995 there were no people of color functioning as CEOs in the Fortune 500. Since that time, many have successfully reached the CEO level and moved beyond, including Lloyd Ward, Franklin Raines, and Ann Fudge, and even with the resignations of Stan O'Neal, Lewis, and Parsons, there remain at least four African American, four Latino, five Asian, and thirteen women who serve as CEOs of Fortune 500 companies, according to *DiversityInc* magazine.*

AFRICAN AMERICAN FORTUNE 500 CEOs
- Rodney O'Neal, Delphi
- Kenneth Chenault, American Express
- Ronald Williams, Aetna
- Clarence Otis, Darden Restaurants

LATINO FORTUNE 500 CEOs
- Antonio Perez, Kodak
- Hector Ruiz, Advanced Micro Devices
- Paul Diaz, Kindred Health Care
- Jose Maria Alapont, Federal-Mogul

---

*"Why Are So Few CEOs People of Color and Women?" *DiversityInc*, November 2007.

ASIAN FORTUNE 500 CEOS
- Indra K. Nooyi, PepsiCo
- Ramani Ayer, Hartford Financial Services
- Andrea Jung, Avon Products
- Rajiv L. Gupta, Rohm and Haas
- Surya N. Mohapatra, Quest Diagnostics

WOMEN FORTUNE 500 CEOS
- Angela Braly, WellPoint
- Patricia Woertz, Archer Daniels Midland
- Indra K. Nooyi, PepsiCo
- Brenda Barnes, Sara Lee
- Mary Sammons, Rite Aid
- Carol Meyrowitz, TJX
- Anne Mulcahy, Xerox
- Patricia Russo, Lucent Technologies
- Susan Ivey, Reynolds American
- Andrea Jung, Avon Products
- Marion O. Sandler, Golden West Financial
- Paula Rosput Reynolds, Safeco
- Margaret Whitman, eBay*

The success of these pioneers should create a sense of hope that others will be groomed and follow in their footsteps—and that the growth in minority representation will only continue to increase as corporations truly come to appreciate the business and economic benefits of truly valuing diverse leadership.

---

*As this book was being written, Margaret Whitman was planning to retire as CEO of eBay Inc. in March 2008.

SO . . . WHAT DID I LEARN?

Recently, after delivering a keynote address for the National Sales Network, I was approached by a young man in the audience who asked a very insightful question: "What changed to allow you to move from being a PoPo [passed over and pissed off] to where you are today?" Though I have shared much of this in the book, I realized a few points were vital in my transformation from where I was to where I am.

Don't expect anyone to promote you . . . until you promote yourself! For the first seven to ten years of my career, I operated on the assumption that if I worked hard, delivered results, and stayed out of harm's way, the bosses would notice me, reward me, and promote me. The reality was, it was my responsibility to make certain, in addition to delivering results, that the right people knew of my performance, and also knew what my career aspirations were. Furthermore, it was up to me to determine what direction or career path I should take. Yes, mentors can assist, sponsors can pave the way, but at the end of the day, I had to be the author and architect of my career.

There are people who will help you . . . and they don't always look like you! One of the ironies of my career is, while I have enjoyed the counsel and guidance of many capable minority mentors, most of the support, encouragement, and sponsorship I have received has been from others who look nothing like myself. It amazed me, the number of people willing to give direction, offer support, and open doors once I took the focus off of what "the man" wasn't doing for me, and allowed myself to be open to feedback, coaching, and direction. I soon began to realize that not every nonminority was against me, looked down on me, or was threatened by me (though more were than were not)—and that there are many senior leaders, of all shapes, sizes, genders, and colors, who actually take great delight in identifying and developing minority talent.

What got me here . . . may not get me where I want to go! For most of us who have achieved any level of success in the corporate world, we have developed certain skills and behaviors that have helped us get to where we are. We have worked hard to cultivate these skills and develop these behaviors, and we *know* how to utilize them to get things done. However, it can be difficult for us to accept the fact that to move from where we are to where we want to be, we may need new skills, new ideas, and different ways of behaving. We falsely assume that what made us successful in the past will make us successful in the future. In his new book, *What Got You Here Won't Get You There*, Marshall Goldsmith discusses how previous accomplishments often prevent otherwise successful people from achieving even greater success. In his book he details twenty-one habits that can keep a leader from reaching the top. I was amazed to see how many of those habits I had developed over the years, and now, thanks to the recommendations he outlines, I have begun to work on those I have yet to change.

To reach your career goals, you may have to take a hard look in the mirror, seek input and feedback from others, and make a commitment to constant self-improvement. This commitment may require you to learn new skills, modify behaviors, and unlearn bad habits. However, you and your career may experience exponential growth as a result.

If you can't be an entrepreneur . . . be an "intra-preneur." At many points in my career I have witnessed dozens of colleagues leave corporate America, frustrated with all of the layoffs, downsizing, right-sizing, and gamesmanship. They concluded that rather than waste energy playing the corporate game, they would become entrepreneurs and use that energy for their own benefit. They would be their own boss, with no one to answer to but themselves. In every case, I would applaud their decision, as I am a firm believer that more minorities should own their own businesses. We should have minority-owned airlines, hotels, grocery stores, retail banks, and other businesses to employ more minorities and keep more minority dollars in minority communities. However, being an entrepreneur is more than just a romantic notion. It requires a great deal of planning, resources, execution, and above all, capital. All too often I would watch as many of these talented individuals became even more frustrated as entrepreneurs and, in most cases, returned to the workforce, many times in positions lower than when they left, at lower salaries.

I attempted to run my own entertainment business on the side while working as a VP in corporate America. After two years of trying to grow too fast, I sold my share of the business and focused my efforts on becoming an "intra-preneur" within the corporate world. Simply put, I was determined to treat my role within my company, regardless of what it was, as if I were running my own business. I would set out to create my own brand, hire and develop my own team, and focus on delivering results as if I were the sole proprietor. I paid closer attention to expenses, as if it were my own money. I made personnel decisions as if I were paying them from my own pocket. And most of all I created an entrepreneurial atmosphere where new ideas were welcome, customer service was king, and success was recognized and rewarded. The net result was, my teams typically worked harder, had more fun, and delivered better results than ever before. What was my reward? I have enjoyed increased levels of compensation, recognition, and responsibility. And since I ran the company as my business, I made sure that women and people of color were given opportunities to develop and grow. My hope is, these same individuals will in turn reach out and help other minorities as they continue to move up the ladder.

NEVER GIVE UP!

Lastly, if I could offer only one piece of advice to all minorities, it would be this: Never give up! While it sounds simple, most minority professionals will tell you that working in corporate environments is anything but simple! The derailment factors listed earlier in the book, of which "difficulty in adapting" and "problems with interpersonal relationships" lead the list, are never too far away, making the climb to the top of the corporate mountain that much more difficult for the minority professional. However, I am a firm believer in the human spirit and the ability of people to rise above their circumstances, their upbringing, and even their failures. In his book *I Can't Accept Not Trying*, basketball superstar Michael Jordan writes of how his being cut from his varsity basketball team as a sophomore served as the motivation for him to ultimately become arguably the sport's best athlete ever. Later, when he speaks of failure, he offers an interesting insight: "I can accept failure. Everyone fails at something. But I can't accept not trying."

During your corporate career, you will experience failure! A presentation will not go well, you may find yourself unprepared for a key meeting, or perhaps you will lose a major client. Failure is inevitable! But as Michael Jordan also states, "failure is an illusion." It only becomes a reality when we let it define who we are. Never give up! Never give up on your goals. Never give up on your dreams. And above all, never give up on yourself! Even when others say you can't achieve it! Even when family and friends can't see it! And even when you feel like giving up is the only alternative. History shows that success is achievable for those who refuse to give up:

- **General MacArthur** was denied admission to West Point—not once but twice. But the third time he applied he was accepted, and marched into the history books!
- **Einstein's** teachers described him as mentally slow, unsociable, and "adrift in his foolish dreams."
- **Enrico Caruso's** music teacher told him he "had no voice at all, and couldn't sing."
- **Michael Jordan** was encouraged to go to the Air Force Academy rather than attending the University of North Carolina because he wouldn't be able to play at that level, and at least if he attended the Air Force Academy, he would have a job!
- **Venus and Serena Williams** weren't taken seriously as tennis players because their father trained them on the public courts of Compton, rather than at world-class tennis facilities.
- **Keith Wyche's** mother was told by his principal that, rather than send him to a private high school, she should save her money and buy a new refrigerator.

Thankfully, none of these people listened to the voices of defeat and went on to accomplish more than they ever dreamed of! And thankfully, my mother decided that it was more important to invest in her son's future than spend my father's hard-earned money on creature comforts. It's an investment that is still paying dividends, and will for years to come!

ACKNOWLEDGMENTS

It would be impossible for me to have my name appear on the cover of this book without taking time to thank those who were instrumental in helping make my dream of writing this book a reality. Above all, I would like to thank God for bringing so many wonderful people into my life, and for making it all possible. To my co-writer, Sonia Alleyne, for her hard work both in helping write the book and in keeping me sane as I obsessed over deadlines! To John C. Maxwell and Jack Canfield, for planting the seed in my heart and encouraging me to write it. Also, special thanks go to George Fraser for not only planting the seed to write the book, but watering and nurturing it by introducing me to the best literary agent in the business, Barbara Lowenstein, and the entire Lowenstein-Yost agency. (By the way, Barbara, thanks for talking me out of the first title I had selected!)

One of the best experiences I had during this whole process was working with my editor, Jillian Gray, and the rest of the Portfolio team: Adrian Zackheim, Adrienne Schultz, Maureen Cole, and Will Weisser. Thanks for not making me feel like the "rookie" writer I was during this process. Jillian, you're the best! Not to be overlooked is my *Good Is Not Enough* marketing and public relations team: Kinetra Smith and Tori Allen of Brainchild Associates, my good friend Charmaine Ward of CW Marketing Consultants, and Paul Robertson of J Dezigns, who worked with me to make sure that my image, visibility, and Web site were first-class. The other member of this team I could not do without is my assistant, the lovely Anne Fleming, who not only keeps me organized on a daily basis but represents me in the most professional manner imaginable when acting on my behalf. Additionally, I must thank my entire Pitney Bowes family, who have supported this effort to the utmost. Other supporters I owe a debt of gratitude to are: Carl Brooks and my Executive Leadership Council family; Bill Wells and Barbara Thomas of the National Black MBA Association; Pam McAlvane of *Diversity MBA* magazine; Dr. Robert Rodriguez of the Hispanic Alliance for Career Enhancement; and David Richardson and the entire National Sales Network family for being the first organization to embrace this book and provide copies to its membership.

The book was also special to me in that I called upon some very talented individuals to contribute their wisdom and insights to help make my ideas and concepts come to life. Thanks to Dr. Lawana Gladney, Dr. Wilbur Sykes, Kim Bianca Williams, David Samuel, and my pastor, Reverend W. Darin Moore. On a more personal note, I would like to thank a great group of guys: Lawrence Lee, Tony Lyons, Ron Broadnax, Mark Ellis, Paul Richardson, Andre Fort, and Curtiss Jacobs, my "inner circle," for keeping me grounded through the years. I also must honor my uncles, Z. Harold Davis, Jr., and Paul Jones, Jr., who, along with my father, the late Leroy Wyche, served as my first and most trusted mentors.

Finally, I must thank my mother, Velvet Wyche, who during my childhood set high standards and never accepted anything less than my best. To my sisters, Valerie Middlebrooks and Karen Wyche, for always being there to support their big brother. Much love and thanks to my children, Alana, Kyle, Kevin, and Angela, for providing the continuing motivation in my life to be the best that I can be. Most of all, thanks to my guardian angel, Carla Maria, who for over thirty-five years has been in my life in so many capacities, as a best friend, wife, mother to my children, and business partner. Thank you for always believing in me, even when I didn't believe in myself.

FURTHER RESOURCES

MANAGEMENT/LEADERSHIP

1. Jack Canfield, *The Success Principles* (New York: HarperCollins, 2005).
2. Ram Charan, *Know-How* (New York: Crown Books, 2007).
3. Marshall Goldsmith, *What Got You Here Won't Get You There* (New York: Hyperion Press, 2007).
4. Oren Harari, *The Leadership Secrets of Colin Powell* (New York: McGraw-Hill, 2002).
5. John C. Maxwell, *The 21 Irrefutable Laws of Leadership* (Nashville, TN: Thomas Nelson Press, 1998, 2007).
6. ———, *Talent Is Never Enough* (Nashville, TN: Thomas Nelson Press, 2007).
7. Sun Tzu, *The Art of War,* ed. James Clavell (New York: Delacorte Press, 1983).
8. Michael Watkins, *The First 90 Days* (Cambridge, MA: Harvard Business School Press, 2003).

MINORITY BUSINESS

1. Price M. Cobbs and Judith L. Turnock, *Cracking the Corporate Code* (New York: Amacom, 2003).
2. Harvey J. Coleman, *Empowering Yourself* (Dubuque, IA: Kendall-Hunt, 1996).

3. Augusto Failde and William Doyle, *Latino Success* (New York: Fireside, 1996).

4. Earl G. Graves, *How to Succeed in Business Without Being White* (New York: HarperCollins, 1997).

5. Jane Hyun, *Breaking the Bamboo Ceiling* (New York: HarperCollins, 2005).

6. Kenneth Arroyo Roldan, *Minority Rules* (New York: HarperCollins, 2006).

7. David A. Thomas and John J. Gabarro, *Breaking Through* (Cambridge, MA: Harvard Business School Press, 1999).

WOMEN'S INTEREST

1. Lois P. Frankel, *Nice Girls Don't Get the Corner Office* (New York: Warner Books, 2004).

2. Pamela F. Lenehan, *What You Don't Know and Your Boss Won't Tell You* (Minneapolis: Syren Books, 2006).

3. Courtney Lynch and Angie Morgan, *Leading from the Front* (New York: McGraw-Hill, 2006).

BUSINESS NETWORKING/RELATIONSHIP MANAGEMENT

1. George C. Fraser, *Click* (New York: McGraw-Hill, 2007).

2. Ronna Lichtenberg, *It's Not Business, It's Personal* (New York: Hyperion, 2001).

3. Cynthia Shapiro, *Corporate Confidential* (New York: St. Martin's Press, 2005).

4. William Ury, *The Power of a Positive No* (New York: Bantam Books, 2007).

MINORITY RECRUITING

1. Robert Rodriguez, *Latino Talent* (Hoboken, NJ: John Wiley & Sons, 2007).

2. Joe Watson, *Without Excuses* (New York: St. Martin's Press, 2006).

PROFESSIONAL BUSINESS ORGANIZATIONS FOR MINORITIES

National Society of Hispanic MBAs
1303 Walnut Hill Lane, Suite 100
Irving, TX 75038
www.nshmba.org
(214) 596-9338

iHispano.com
4265 N. Knox Ave., Suite 300
Chicago, IL 60641
www.ihispano.com
(888) 252-1220

Association of Latino Professionals in
   Finance and Accounting (ALPFA)
801 South Grand Ave., Suite 400
Los Angeles, CA 90017
www.alpfa.org
(213) 243-0004

Executive Leadership Council (ELC)
1001 North Fairfax Street, Suite 300
Alexandria, VA 22314
www.elcinfo.com
(703) 706-5212

National Association of Black
   Accountants (NABA)
7249-A Hanover Parkway
Greenbelt, MD 20770
www.nabainc.org
(301) 474-NABA

National Sales Network (NSN)
3695 F Cascade, Suite 2184
Atlanta, GA 30331
www.salesnetwork.org
(404) 629-4418

Hispanic Alliance for Career
   Advancement
(HACE)
25 E. Washington, Suite 820
Chicago, IL 60602
www.hace-usa.org
(312) 435-0498

National Hispanic Business
   Association
(NHBA)
5766 Balcones Dr., Suite 203
Austin, TX 78731
www.NHBA.org
(512) 380-7575

National Black MBA Association
(NBMBAA)
180 North Michigan Ave.
Chicago, IL 60601
www.nbmbaa.org
(312) 236-2622

Black Data Processing Association
(BDPA)
6301 Ivy Lane, Suite 700
Greenbelt, MD 20770
www.bdpa.org
(800) 727-BDPA

National Society of Black Engineers
(NSBE)
205 Dangerfield Rd.
Alexandria, VA 22314
www.nsbe.org
(703) 549-2207

Frasernet
2940 Noble Road, Suite 1
Cleveland Heights, OH 44121
www.frasernet.com
(216) 691-6686

National Association of Black
Telecommunications Professionals
2020 Pennsylvania Ave., NW, Box 735
Washington, DC 20006
www.naptp.org
(800) 946-6228

Catalyst
120 Wall St., 5th Fl.
New York, NY 10005
www.catalyst.org
(212) 514-7600

Leadership Education for Asian Pacifics
327 East 2nd St., Suite 226
Los Angeles, CA 90012
www.leap.org
(213) 485-1422

Society of Women Engineers (SWE)
230 East Ohio St., Suite 400
Chicago, IL 60611
www.swe.org
(312) 596-5223

American Business Women's
Association
9100 Ward Parkway, P.O. Box 8728
Kansas City, MO 64114-0728
www.abwa.org
(800) 228-0007

National Association of Asian
American Professionals
P.O. Box 50958
Palo Alto, CA 94303
www.naaap.org
(650) 333-9533

INDEX

accountability, 106
accounting scandals, 85
adaptability, 106
advancement
    career blueprint and, 64–71
    corporate culture and, 13–14
    distractions from, 75–76
    exit strategies and, 26–27
    identifying help for, 78–80
    lateral moves vs., 58–59
    missing opportunities for, 60–61
    passions and, 74–75
    personality traits and, 72–74
    presentation skills and, 117–18
    questions to ask, 21
    relocation and, 66–68
    self-knowledge and, 71–72, 77–78
    size of organization and, 62–64
    skill set and, 76–77
    switching industries and, 84
    visibility and, 44–47, 48–49
advisors, 158
Aetna, 29
African Americans
    CEO percentage, 9

compensation among, 211
    in criminal justice system, 212
    dropout rates among, 212
    Fortune 500 CEOs, 221
    incarceration of, 212
    poverty among, 211
    in special education, 211
    unemployment of, 211
    young male, outlook for, 211–13
Ameritech, 32–33, 34
analytical thinking, 119–21
annual report, as research material,
    20
Asian Americans
    CEO percentage, 9
    Fortune 500 CEOs, 222
    organizations for, 216
assumed competence, 35
awareness
    of corporate culture, 11–12
    as executive skill, 106

Bank of America, 23
belief, in oneself, 24–25
blueprint, career, 64–71

boards of directors, African Americans in, 10
Bossidy, Larry, 128
bottom-line focus, 100
bragging, *vs.* visibility, 41–42
branding. *see* personal branding

"C players," 134–35
Caputo, Carol, 133
career blueprint, 64–71
career derailment
    definition of, 90
    feedback and, 95–98
    performance expectations and, 92–95
    value quantification and, 99–104
career killers, unethical behavior, 86–88
Center for Creative Leadership (CCL), 90
CEO(s)
    African American, 221
    Asian American, 222
    as career goal, 70–71
    female, 222
    Latino American, 221
    minority representation as, 9–10
    number of minority, 8
Charan, Ram, 128
Charles Dickens Elementary School, 133
Chenault, Ken, 42–43, 128–30, 221
child support, among Latino Americans, 214
Cingular, 57
clarity, in communication, 113–14
Clarke, Caroline V., 42–43
coaches, executive, 146–47
code of conduct violations, 89
collaboration, 36
communication
    clarity in, 113–14
    concise, 113
    conversation skills and, 179–80
    as executive skill, 111–16
    oral, 112–14
    in presentations, 116–19
    written, 114–16
compensation
    among African Americans, 211
    questions to ask, 21

competence
    assumed, 35
    demonstrated, 34–35
    in leadership, 46–47
competition
    continuous learning and, 177–79
    retention and, 105
concise communication, 113
consensus building, 121–25
continuous learning
    competition and, 177–79
    diverse paths to, 184–85
    focus on talent and, 173–77
    industry organizations and, 183
    industry publications and, 183–84
    new language acquisition and, 184
    reading and, 183
conversation skills, 179–80
corporate culture
    advancement and, 13–14
    awareness of, 11–12
    "fit" and, 15
    mentors and, 193
    rewards and, 16
    rituals and, 15–16
    seniority and, 16–17
    size and, 17–18
    unethical behavior and, 87–88
courage, 129
criminal justice system, African Americans in, 212
Critelli, Michael J., 172
critical success factors (CSFs), 104
C.S.I. (television show), 150
culture. *see* corporate culture

deciphering responses, 186–87
demonstrated competence, 34–35
Detroit Hispanic Development Corporation, 213–15
discrimination
    fear of, 187
    reality of, 23
distraction, 75–76
diversity
    questions to ask about, 20–21
    rhetoric *vs.* reality, 21–22
"diversity hires," 32

dress
  culture and, 187–88
  perception and, 31–34
Dress for Success (Malloy), 31
DuBois, W. E. B., 209

early education, 133–34
education. *see* continuous learning
emotion
  vs. passion, 164–65
  women and, 161–62
emotional preparedness, 148–51
engagement, women and, 170
Enron, 85
events, company, 55
executive coaches, 146–47
Executive Leadership Council (ELC),
  123–25, 200–202
executive presence, 31–34
executive-level skills
  communication as, 111–16
  execution as, 127–28
  financial skills as, 126–27
  leadership in, 110
  overview of, 106–7
  problem solving as, 119–21
  stakeholder management as, 121–25
  varying, 109–10
  vs. sales skills, 107–9
exit strategy
  definition of, 25–26
  importance of, 25
  tips for, 27
experience
  career blueprint and, 68–70
  lateral moves and, 57–58
  leveraging of, 192
  of mentors, 197

Fannie Mae, 85
feedback, career derailment and, 95–98
financial skills, 126–27
first impressions, 32, 112. *see also*
  personal branding
fit, culture and, 15
flexibility, 106, 168
Flynn, Nancy, 114
"followership," 36

forces, impacting success, 125
formality, of mentor relationships,
  190–91
fraud, 87–88
Fudge, Ann, 221

General Electric, 23
giving back, 217–19
goals
  awareness of, 77–78
  keeping sight of, 80–83
  sponsors and, 193–95
Godfather, The, 157
gold stars, 52–53

Hart, Seitu Jemel, 217–19
Harvey, George, 184–85
health, among Latino Americans, 214
high-school dropout rates, among
  African Americans, 212
Hispanic Executive Summit, 200. *see also*
  National Society of Hispanic MBAs
  (NSHMBA)

illegal activity, 87–88
incarceration
  of African Americans, 212
  of Latino Americans, 215
industry organizations, 183
industry switching, 84
informality, of mentor relationships,
  190–91
information decoders, mentors as,
  190–93
Institute for Leadership Development
  and Research, 200–201. *see also*
  Executive Leadership Council (ELC)
integrity, 88, 129, 154–55
Internet, impact of, 172
interpersonal skills, 123
interviews, preparation for, 140–43
"intra-preneur," 225

Kodak, 81

labor participation, of Latino Americans,
  215
languages, learning new, 184

lateral moves
  experience and, 57–58
  vs. advancing moves, 58–59
Latino Americans
  CEO percentage, 9
  child support among, 214
  Fortune 500 CEOs, 221
  health among, 214
  incarceration of, 215
  labor participation of, 215
  medical insurance among, 214
  poverty among, 214
  unemployment among, 215
Leaders of Tomorrow program, 199
leadership
  as executive skill, 106, 110
  integrity and, 154–55
  perseverance and, 155–56
  "VIPs" of, 153–56
  vision and, 153–54
leadership competencies, 46–47
Leadership Institute, 198–99
leadership quotient, 35–37
learning. *see* continuous learning
leveraging, of experience, 192
Lewis, Aylwin, 8, 19, 221
Lichtenberg, Ronna, 164
limitations, by others, 24–25
location, career blueprint and, 66–68

Madison, Paula, 191
majority, minorities as, 176–77
Martin, Murray, 128–29, 180–81
Mauborgne, Renée, 181–82
MBAs, increasing number of, 179
McCann, Renetta, 157
McDonald's USA, 131
medical insurance, among Latino
  American children, 214
mental preparedness, 144–48
mentors
  corporate culture and, 13–14, 193
  developing relationship, 189–90
  experience of, 197
  identities of, 188–89
  importance of, 188–90
  as information decoders, 190–93
  mentee qualities and, 196–97

  multiple, 197, 233
  organizational, 198–202
  preparation and, 202–3
  relationship with, 198
  risks and, 196–97
  scheduling and, 203
  signing on of, 195–98
Merrill Lynch, 8
minorities, as majorities, 176–77
minority imperative, 208–10
Molloy, John, 31
Moore, Reverend W. Darin, 152–53

National Black MBA Association
  (NBMBAA), 20, 78, 176, 198–99
National Coalition for Asian Pacific
  American Community
  Development, 216–17
National Sales Network (NSN), 176
National Society of Hispanic MBAs
  (NSHMBA), 20, 176, 199–200
National Urban League (NUL), 176
networking
  personal branding and, 38–39
  as research, 22
  women and, 169–70
NextGen Network, 201–2. *see also*
  Executive Leadership Council (ELC)

offshoring, 178–79
Omega Psi Phi Fraternity, 210–13
O'Neal, Stanley, 8, 221
opponents, 159
opportunity, making most of, 181–82
oral communication, 112–14
organizational mentoring, 198–202
outsourcing, 178–79

Parsons, Richard, 8, 75
passion
  importance of knowing, 74–75
  vs. emotion, 164–65
perception. *see* personal branding
performance, *vs.* seniority, 16–17
performance expectations, 92–95
performance rating, visibility and, 45–47
performance reviews, 53, 96, 140–41
perseverance, 155–56, 226–27

personal branding
    collaboration and, 36
    definition of, 30
    demonstrated competence and, 34–35
    dress and, 31–34
    goal of, 30–31
    leadership and, 35–37
    networking and, 38–39
    phases of, 37–39
    portfolio for, 38
    stereotypes and, 30
personality traits, 72–74
Pitney Bowes, 23
planning, preparation and, 137–38
political judgment, 106, 169
Porter, Michael, 121
portfolio, personal, 38
poverty
    among African Americans, 211
    among Latino Americans, 214
preparation
    emotional, 148–51
    importance of, 132
    for interviews, 140–43
    mastery and, 139
    mental, 144–48
    mentors and, 202–3
    planning and, 137–38
    for presentations, 138
    risks of unpreparedness, 135–37
    spiritual, 151–53
presentations
    preparing for, 138
    rehearsing, 139
    skills for, 116–19
Prince, Don W., 90, 91
problem-solving skills, 119–21
process, in male vs. female thought,
    164–65
progress, of minorities, 8–10
promotion. see advancement
publications, industry, 183–84

quantification, of value, 99–104
questions
    of employer by employee, 18–22
    preparing, 140
quid pro quo, 159–60

racism, 186–87
Raines, Franklin, 85
ranking, visibility and, 49–50
reading, continuous learning and,
    183
regulations, 172
rehearsing presentations, 139
relocation, 66–68
research
    networking as, 22
    pre-hire, 18–22
responses, deciphering of, 186–87
responsibility, 23–24
restraining forces, 125
retention, 105
rewards, corporate culture and, 16
Reyes, Angie, 213
rituals, corporate culture and, 15–16

sales skills, vs. management skills,
    107–9
Samuel, David, 51
Sandler, Debra, 170
scheduling, with mentors, 203
Sears Holdings, 8
second chances, lack of, 86
self-knowledge, 71–72
senior management
    as career goal, 70–71
    visibility to, 53–54
seniority, vs. performance, 16–17
sexual harassment, 87–88
Shanahan, Betty, 217–19
significance, vs. success, 206–7
Singh, Jasbinder, 89–90
size, of corporation
    advancement and, 62–64
    corporate culture and, 17–18
skill set, at various levels, 109–10
skill set assessment, 76–77
skip-level meeting, 98
social responsibility, 172
Sonnenfeld, Jeffrey A., 85
Sony Ericsson, 160
special education, among African
    Americans, 211
speech, 112–14
spiritual preparation, 151–53

sponsors. *see also* mentors
　developing relationship with,
　　189–90
　identities of, 188–89
　importance of, 188–90
　as quarterbacks to goal, 193–95
　signing on of, 195–98
sports, 8
stakeholder management, 121–25
stereotypes
　communication and, 111
　emotion and, 148–49
　perception and, 30
strategic thought, 37, 46–47, 106
strengths
　knowing, 71–72
　tailoring to, 72–73
success, *vs.* significance, 206–7
"sucking up" *vs.* visibility, 44
supervisor support, 168
switching industries, 84
Sykes, Wilbert R., 146

talent, increased corporate focus on,
　175–77
Target, 23
Thomas, Clarence, 209
Thomas, David A., 189
Thompson, Donald, 131
Time Warner/AOL, 8
timeline, exit strategy and, 27
trajectory, 189
T-shirt metaphor, 51–52

unemployment
　of African Americans, 211
　of Latino Americans, 215
unethical behavior, 86–88
unique minority of one (UMO), 146,
　147–48

unpreparedness, 135–37
Urban Arts Academy Alternative High
　School, 214

value quantification, 99–104
VIPs, of leadership, 153–56
visibility
　advancement and, 44–47, 48–49
　company events and, 55
　importance of, 44–47
　minority advantages in, 42–43
　performance rating and, 45–47
　performance reviews and, 53
　personal branding and, 39
　pitfalls in, 40–42
　ranking and, 49–50
　to senior management, 53–54
　volunteering and, 55
　vs. bragging, 41–42
　vs. sucking up, 44
vision, leadership and, 153–54
volunteering
　opportunity and, 78–80
　visibility and, 55

Watkins, Michael, 142
weaknesses, knowing, 71–72
Wellington, Sheila, 190
Williams, Kim Bianca, 196
Williams, Ronald A., 29–30
women
　barriers to success of, 165–66
　CEO percentage, 9
　emotions and, 161–62
　engagement and, 170
　networking and, 169–70
　politics and, 169
work, importance of, 22–23
WorldCom, 85
written communication, 114–116